The Train
of the]

Catherine Sutton

John Bartholomew & Son Limited
Edinburgh

First published in Great Britain 1980 by
John Bartholomew & Son Limited
12 Duncan Street, Edinburgh, EH9 1TA

© John Bartholomew & Son Limited 1980

ISBN 0 7028 8030 2
1st edition
Reprinted 1982, 1984

Sutton, Catherine
  The training and care of the family dog. -
  (Bartholomew pet series)
  1. Dogs
  I. Title
  636.7'08'3

Printed in Great Britain by
John Bartholomew & Son Limited

Contents

If the history of all the dogs who have loved and been loved by the race of man could be written each history of a dog would resemble all the other histories. It would be a love story.

James Douglas

Selecting a Breed

The care of any family dog really starts before one even owns him. It is the prospective owner's responsibility to make quite sure that the dog chosen is best suited for whatever facilities and general care can be given to the animal. For instance, it is no good deciding to have a Great Dane or an Irish Wolfhound if the space available is a town flat. Similarly, although Afghans, Poodles, and Old English Sheepdogs — well groomed ones — are the admiration of most people, it must be remembered that keeping their coats in good condition requires a great deal of time and work. There are many grooming parlours that will take on the job of caring for your dog's coat, but surely it is not too much to ask that between attendances the owner grooms his dog and keeps the coat free of mats and tangled hair. It is quite surprising how many people forget the discomforts of the dog when the novelty of owning a glamorous pet fades. I have seen, on many occasions, dogs so badly matted that the only answer has been to clip the whole coat off — just like a sheep. Very sad, but so true.

If one is not prepared to give a long-coated dog proper care and attention, then surely the best idea is to purchase a dog that presents no problems in this respect.

With the breeds that require to be clipped and stripped from time to time, one must be prepared for a certain outlay to enable the dog to have this service from professional dog beauticians. These people will request that the dog be brought regularly for attention, for if left too long in between strips it is more difficult to do and takes a longer time. Even most terriers need their coats trimmed or stripped about twice a year, when the coat is dead. This should be done mainly by hand and it is essential that the dead coat should come out, otherwise the dog will start scratching and sores will appear.

Most dogs cast their coat twice a year. If this is going to annoy anyone in your household, even with all the many household gadgets that will soon collect up the hair, then perhaps you should consider a breed that is less likely to lose so much coat.

GREYHOUNDS	HOUNDS	GUN DOGS		GUARD DOGS
Afgan	Basset	Bloodhound	Labrador	Boxer
Borzoi	Beagle	Cocker Spaniel	Norfolk Spaniel	Doberman
English Greyhound	Bloodhound	English Setter	Pointer	Great Dane
Irish Wolfhound	Foxhound	German Pointer	Springer Spaniel	Newfoundland
Saluki		Golden Retriever	Weimeraner	St. Bernard
Whippet		Irish Setter		

HUNTING DOGS

8

SHEPHERD DOGS

Alsatian

Collie

Old English Shepherd Dog

Pyrenean Mountain Dog

Shetland Sheep Dog

TERRIERS

Airedale Terrier

Daschund

Bedlington Terrier

Scottish Terrier

Boston Terrier

Smooth-haired Terrier

Bull Terrier

Staffordshire Bull Terrier

Cairn Terrier

West Highland White Terrier

Corgi

Wire-haired Fox Terrier

PET DOGS

Bulldog

Pug

Chihuahua

Schipperke

Dalmatian

Yorkshire Terrier

Pekingese

Pomeranian

Poodle

WORKING DOGS   PET DOGS

The coated dogs all have a certain amount of glamour, but they also place a great responsibility on their owners to see that coats are at all times properly cared for. Depending on the breed this can take quite a lot of time and every so often a professional's time to clip the coat. The long-coated dogs are more work than the short-coated dogs. No one can deny this. Take a long-coated dog for a walk across a park or field on a wet muddy day and on returning he needs not just a quick rub down with a towel but, in fairness to the dog, a grooming to get rid of all the dirt and mud that may have collected in his coat. This is usually done when the coat has dried off. Do be assured that all the work spent on a dog's coat is never wasted, and apart from the fact that your dog will very much appreciate being kept in good condition, for those who enjoy this sort of task it is very rewarding. If you are prepared for this work there is a wide range of breeds open to you for consideration. You may even learn to strip and clip the animal yourself.

Characters in dogs vary from breed to breed and, of course, from dog to dog. If you are not as agile as you used to be and not prepared for long walks on most days of the week, it is wise to settle for a smaller dog. Because of their size this does not mean that they lack character. Some of the smaller dogs simply ooze character whereas some of the larger varieties can be lacking in this. In my opinion, character is an important quality for a family dog to possess. After all, a human with a sense of humour is surely much easier to live with than one who has none at all.

Having selected your breed you must then decide whether you are going to buy a male or a female. I feel that this choice is entirely up to the individual. It may be that you want to breed at a later stage, so this immediately solves your dilemma, but if you just want a companion, there is much to say in favour of both dogs and bitches. We all know there is perhaps a little inconvenience when the bitch comes into season and she has to be kept under lock and key, particularly when she is ready to be mated. However there are many proprietory remedies on the market today that can help disguise this situation so that, with care on the owner's part, there need be no dramas. If you find that you are unable to cope with your bitch when she is in season, perhaps because of uninvited guests, then you can always place her in a good boarding kennel where they are well equipped to deal with such a situation.

In making a choice between dog and bitch it is well to remember that dogs are generally bigger than bitches. Some say that bitches are better with children and on the whole more affectionate. I do not agree as I have had both sexes in different breeds as my personal companions and have certainly found no fault with either. They have been equally loyal and loveable, with charming characters, and at all times good with my family.

As a general rule I feel that a companion dog for a young family should be a rather sturdy, hardy type of animal; adventurous but with a good steady temperament and no sign of shyness or distrustfulness. Most well-brought-up dogs are faithful to their family and/or owner but, of course, in every breed, as in some families, there are rogues that few can train.

Big dogs are no more difficult to train than small dogs. In fact, I would say that often they are easier to train but, of course, an unmanageable large dog is more trouble than an untrained little one. An untrained little dog can be a perfect nuisance but an untrained large one can be a complete menace, not only to his family but to the public at large.

In the hope of being helpful to those who are just about to own a dog for the first time, or wish to replace a dear old pet that has died, there follows a list of all the breeds that are recognized by the Kennel Club. These breeds are all given Championship status. Apart from these there are many other breeds that have been imported but do not yet have quite enough registrations to join the Championship list. If you want to delve into these breeds, known at the moment as 'rare breeds', further information can be obtained from the Kennel Club, which will be pleased to put you in touch with the Breed Club Secretary who can give you further information about the particular breed. However, with over one hundred breeds listed here from which to select, this wide choice should enable you to make a happy decision as to your future companion dog.

Having made your final choice, please always remember that *you* chose your dog; he did not choose you. It is therefore your responsibility to see that all his needs are attended to, and if done, I am sure he or she will repay you with the love and devotion that only a dog can give his master.

Gundogs

Members of this group of dogs, as the name implies, are suitable for training to the gun. Obviously they need a good deal of exercise, particularly the Setters, Retrievers, and Pointers. They are usually kind, gentle animals with a desire to please and are easily trained as house pets. None of them, except perhaps the American Cocker Spaniel, have excessive coats to deal with.

English Setter: An elegant dog with working ability. Coat long and silky. Height: 25–27in (64–68.5cm).
German Short Haired Pointer: All-purpose gundog. Coat is short. Height: 23–25in (58–63.5cm).
Gordon Setter: Biggest and heaviest of the Setters and a little more reserved than other Setters. Height: 26in (66cm).
Hungarian Vizsla: National dog of Hungarian sportsmen. Easily

trained. Coat is short. Height: 22−25in (56−63.5cm).

Irish Setter: A very racy, handsome dog with a rich-mahogany, silky coat with feathering. Height: about 25in (64cm).

Pointer: As his name suggests, he points out the game. Loves the scope of open country. Short smooth coat. Height: 25−27in (63.5−68.5cm).

Retriever, Curly-Coated: Coat is one mass of small curls all over — needs careful grooming. Height: 25−27in (63.5−68.5cm).

Retriever, Flat-Coated: Bright, active dog of medium size. Coat dense and as flat as possible. Weight: 60−68lb (27−31kg).

Retriever, Golden: A powerful dog with charming expression who makes a very good companion. Has a flat, golden coat with feathering. Height: 22−24in (56−61cm).

Retriever, Labrador: Has a short dense coat that is easily kept. A very amenable dog that is easily trained. Height: 22−22½in (56−57cm).

Spaniel, American Cocker: His dense coat needs careful stripping and trimming. Usually has a merry, happy disposition. Height: 14−15in (35.5−38cm).

Spaniel, Clumber: A very massive dog for his size. Has a very thoughtful expression and an abundant coat. Weight: 55−70lb (25−32kg).

Spaniel, Cocker: Most popular of all the spaniels. Coat flat and silky with feathering. Height: 15−16in (39−41cm).

Labrador Retriever

Springer Spaniel

Spaniel, English Springer: His coat is close, straight, and weather-resistant. An upstanding merry dog built for endurance and activity. Height: 20in (51cm).

Spaniel, Field: Not so common as other spaniels, but he is a noble, upstanding, sporting dog of lovely temperament. His flat coat is sufficiently dense to resist weather. Height: 18in (46cm).

Spaniel, Irish Water: A great character; loves to belong to one person. His coat is composed of tight, crisp ringlets. Height: 22–24in (56–61cm).

Spaniel, Sussex: Massive and well-built. When on the move has a decided roll. Good family dog. Height: 15–16in (38–40cm).

Spaniel, Welsh Springer: A compact, strong, merry dog, and very active too. Coat straight and thick. Height: 19in (48cm).

Weimeraner: This fearless dog requires careful handling. Protective to his master. Coat short, smooth, and sleek. Height: 24–27in (61–69cm).

Hounds

This group is composed of hunting dogs that hunt either by scent or sight. Like Gundogs they need a fair amount of exercise, particularly the larger breeds. The smaller hounds are readily accepted as house pets and make good companions.

Afghan Hound: Perhaps the most glamorous in this group with his dense long coat and aristocratic bearing. Coat needs careful grooming. Height: 27–29in (68–73cm).

13

Afghan Hound

Basenji: A very smart, short-coated dog. Very rarely barks but can howl. Height: 17in (43cm).

Basset Hound: Can be the family clown, but also a great companion and friend. Short close coat. Height: 13–15in (33–38cm).

Beagle: A very popular hound whose sturdy character makes him a good pet. His short coat is easy to keep. Height: 13–16in (33–40.5cm).

Bloodhound: A big short-coated hound who enjoys his hunting. A great tracker but can be rather reserved. Height: 25–27in (63.5–68.5cm).

Borzoi: A dog that comes from Russia. A most elegant sight-hound. Coat long and silky. Height: from 29in (73.5cm) upwards.

Dachshund: There are six varieties of this breed in the U.K.: *Standard Smooth, Miniature Smooth, Standard Long Haired, Miniature Long Haired, Wire Haired* and *Miniature Wire Haired.* All the varieties require little exercise and make excellent house pets. The miniatures must weigh under 11lb (5.5kg) and the standards over 11lb (5.5kg) up to about 18lb (9kg).

Deerhound: As his name implies he is used to hunt deer. A large loyal dog with a wonderful temperament. Coat harsh and wiry. Height: not less than 30in (76cm).

Elkhound: From Norway, he is used to hunt the Elk in his own country. Thick and abundant coat. Height: 20in (51cm).

Finnish Spitz: A dog that is eager to hunt and has courage and fidelity. Comes originally from Finland. Height: 17in (44cm).

Basset Hound

Greyhound: One of the most ancient breeds. Has great speed in the chase. Has a fine and close coat. Height: 27−30in (71−76cm).

Ibizan Hound: Came originally from the island of Ibiza. A tireless hunter and a kind of dog that is cautious with strangers. Coat either smooth or rough. Height: 23−28in (59−71cm).

Irish Wolfhound: Largest of all existing breeds and a complete gentleman. Rough-coated hound, dependable and loyal. Minimum height: 31in (78.7cm).

Pharaoh Hound: This hound is of great antiquity. Graceful, powerful, and can move with great speed. Coat short. Height: 22−25in (56−63cm).

Rhodesian Ridgeback: Native of South Africa. Capable of great endurance, he was originally used to hunt big game. His coat is short and dense. Height: 27−30in (71−76cm).

Saluki: A most dignified and graceful hound. Rather reserved but very faithful to his family. Coat smooth. Height: 23−28in (58−71cm).

Whippet: A charming smaller hound who makes an excellent companion. Very even tempered. Likes his exercise. Coat is fine and close. Height: 18in (46cm).

Terriers
All of these dogs make excellent companions and are suitable as family dogs. Some of them need to have their coats attended to at least twice a year to strip out the old coat and let the new come in. It is sometimes said, 'once a terrier owner, always a terrier owner'.

Airedale Terrier: Known as the King of Terriers he is nonetheless a very affectionate dog. Makes an excellent guard. Coat needs professional attention. Height: 23−24in (58−61cm).

Australian Terrier: A low-set, compact dog who is very active. Coat needs regular grooming. Height: 10in (25cm).

Bedlington Terrier: Graceful, muscular dog with no coarseness. His thick linty coat needs trimming and regular grooming. Height: 16in (41cm).

Border Terrier: A very spirited dog who makes an ideal companion. Coat is easy to cope with. He is a hardy, pleasing dog with an otterhead. Weight: 13−15lb (6−7kg).

Bull Terrier: Known as the Gladiator of the canine race, he is strongly built and very muscular. Although inclined to fight with other dogs, he can make an excellent family companion.

Miniature Bull Terrier: Like the Bull Terrier but in miniature. Height: must not be more than 14in (36cm).

Cairn Terrier: Comes from the Highlands of Scotland. A happy, gay dog and a very popular pet. His coat requires trimming. Weight: 13lb (6kg).

Dandie Dinmont Terrier: Long-bodied, short-legged terrier. Coat needs careful grooming. Makes a good pet. Height: 8−11in (20−28cm).

Fox Terrier: Two varieties: *Wire* and *Smooth*. *Wire* needs to be groomed and trimmed. Lively and strong dogs. Height: 15in (39cm).

Irish Terrier: Full of temperament and often reckless. Harsh, wiry coat needs trimming. Height: 18in (46cm).

Kerry Blue Terrier: Another Irishman whose temperament can be spirited. His blue-coloured wavy coat is soft and silky and must be carefully trimmed. Height: 18−19in (46−48cm).

Lakeland Terrier: Comes from the English Lake District and is fearless in temperament. Coat needs trimming. Height: not to exceed 14in (36cm).

Manchester Terrier: Black/tan terrier with a smooth coat. Height: 16in (41cm).

Norfolk Terrier: A gay, smart, little, rough-coated dog and a demon for his size. Makes a good house-dog and pet. Height: 9in (25cm).

Norwich Terrier: Similar to the Norfolk but with prick ears. Another dog with spirited character. Height: 9in (25cm).

Scottish Terrier: A very popular terrier. A sturdy thick-set dog. His coat needs trimming. Height: 9−11in (25−28cm).

Sealyham Terrier: Comes from Wales and has a profuse, nearly all-white coat which needs attention. Height: 12in (30cm).

Skye Terrier: From the Isle of Skye. A long-backed dog that prefers to be owned by one person and is therefore rather distrustful of strangers. Coat needs regular grooming. Height: 9in (25cm).

Soft-Coated Wheaten Terrier: From Ireland, very hardy and built on sensible lines. His abundant coat needs attention. Height: 18–19in (46–49cm).

Welsh Terrier: Comes from Wales, resembles a miniature Airedale, and has a lovely temperament. Coat needs trimming. Height: 15in (38cm).

West Highland White Terrier: Comes from Scotland and is a very popular terrier. His white coat needs trimming. Height: 11in (28cm).

Toy Dogs

All the Toy breeds make excellent pets and companions for those who do not want too much exercise. All of the breeds are very happy to be housed with their owners and love their companionship. Most are great characters.

Cavalier King Charles Spaniel: This is a very sporting Toy and capable of enjoying long walks. Coat rather long and silky. Weight: 11–17lb (5–8kg).

Chihauhau: Both long- and short-coated varieties. This is a diminutive breed and weighs from 2–4lb (1–2kg).

English Toy Terrier: Miniature form of the Manchester Terrier. Short, smooth coat. Weight: 6–8lb (3–4kg).

Griffon Bruxellois: The Bruxellois has a rough coat. The Petit Brabancon is smooth-coated. Great characters, very intelligent and active. Weight: 4–11lb (2–5kg).

Italian Greyhound: A miniature Greyhound with real elegance and grace. Enjoys the sun and warmth. Lovely companion. Weight: 5½–8lb (2.5–3.5kg).

Japanese Chin: A very decorative and dainty breed. Has a profuse coat. Weight: about 6½lb (3kg).

King Charles Spaniel: Compact, cobby dog with a very short nose that is upturned. Coat long and silky. Weight: 8–13lb (3.5–6kg).

Löwchen: Often referred to as the Little Lion Dog because the body is clipped like a lion. An intelligent dog that makes a good companion. Weight: 8–9lb (3.5–4kg).

Maltese: From Malta originally. A sweet-tempered dog with long silky-white coat. Makes a lovely companion. Height: not over 9in (25cm).

Miniature Pinscher: A well-balanced, sturdy little dog with a smooth coat. Lots of spirit. Height: 9–12in (25–30cm).

Papillon: Dainty little dog with a lovely head and butterfly ears. Very active and loves attention. Height: 8—11in (20—28cm).

Pekingese: A small thick-set dog of dignity and quality. Needs a minimum of exercise and makes an ideal pet. His profuse coat needs constant attention. Weight: 11lb (5kg).

Pomeranian: A compact dog with a foxy expression. His long overcoat covers the whole of his body. Weight: 3—4lb (1.5—2kg).

Pug: Often described as *multum in parvo* because he is a square dog. He is short-faced with a curled tail and has great character. Weight: 13—17lb (6—8kg).

Yorkshire Terrier: This very active little dog is very popular. His long coat needs careful grooming. Weight: up to 6lb (3kg).

Yorkshire Terrier

Utility Group

This group contains the Poodle family, the Schnauzer family, Tibetan breeds, and others that are not generally looked upon as working breeds. All the dogs in this group make good companions.

Boston Terrier: A native American dog who makes a very good companion for those who have little space to offer. Very strong character, short coat. Weight: not more than 25lb (11.5kg).

Bulldog: A smooth-coated, thick-set dog and a charming, good-natured animal. His appearance belies his character. Weight: 55lb (25kg).

Chow Chow: A Chinese breed and rather an aloof dog. Leonine in appearance; very heavily coated. Height: 18in (45.5cm).

Dalmation: A very sporting dog that loves plenty of exercise. Nonetheless a clean type of dog with a very short coat. Makes a good companion. Height: 23−24in (58−61cm).

French Bulldog: A charming dog with bat ears. Good temperament. Tends to snore rather loudly. Does not require a lot of exercise. Weight: 28lb (12.5kg).

Keeshond: This smart, alert dog from Holland has a fox-like head and a dense coat with profuse trousers. Very affectionate to his family. Height: 18in (45.5cm).

Lhasa Apso: From Tibet, he is a solid dog with a jaunty movement. His profuse coat needs careful grooming. Height: 10in (25cm).

A cream poodle puppy in trim acceptable for showing up to one year old.

Poodle: Comes in three sizes: the Standard, the Miniature, and the Toy. The coat never sheds but it needs to be carefully and regularly clipped. Poodles make lovely pets and companions. Height: from 15in (38cm) and over, down to under 11in (28cm).

Schipperke: Comes from Belgium and makes a very good companion. He is a cobby dog who is very active. His coat is abundant. Height: 12−13in (30.5−33cm).

Schnauzer: Three sizes: Giant, Standard, and Miniature. Their coats are hard and wiry and require stripping. They make good guards. Heights: Giant 25−27in (64−69cm), Standard 19in (48cm), and Miniature 14in (35cm).

Shih Tzus: These are charming, very intelligent, but arrogant little dogs from Tibet, full of their own importance. Their coats are long and dense. Height: not more than 10in (26cm).

Tibetan Spaniel: Also from Tibet. A charming small dog that is gay and very intelligent. Makes a first-rate companion. Height: 10in (25.5cm).

Tibetan Terrier: Another dog from Tibet. Double-coated, with a compact and powerful body. Height: 14−16in (35−40cm).

Working Dogs

This is the biggest group of all six and, as its name implies, the dogs have all been used as working dogs. They all have their own individual qualities and characters and very many of them make excellent companions and guards. They nearly all need a good deal of exercise to keep them fit and happy.

Bearded Collie: This charming dog has a very reliable temperament. He is a good working dog and makes an ideal family companion. His coat needs regular attention. Height: 25−27in (64−69cm).

Belgian Shepherd Dog (Groenendael): Best-known of the Belgian Shepherd Dogs. They are sheepdogs at heart and good guard dogs. Very active and lively on the move. Height: 24−26in (61−66cm).

Bernese Mountain Dog: With his lovely colouring, a most attractive dog. Originates in Switzerland. Used as a draught dog in his home country. Coat soft and silky. Height: 26−27in (66−68cm).

Boxer: A very popular dog with lively spirit and temperament. Coat short and smooth. Tremendous guard for his family. Has great character. Height: 9−10in (22−24cm).

Briard: From France and of rugged appearance. A lively dog full of character. His coat must not be less than 3in (7.5cm) on body. Height: 23−27in (58.5−68.5cm).

Bullmastiff: A very strong, bold dog and a great guard. Coat short and hard. Lovely family dog. Height: 25−27in (63−68cm).

Collie: In two varieties: the Rough Coat and the Smooth. The Rough needs thorough and regular grooming. They enjoy both life outside and life by the fireside. Height: 22−24in (56−61cm).

Dobermann: From Germany he is a tough boy that needs careful handling. Trained properly he is a great guard and loves family life. Short coat. Height: 27in (69.5cm).

A fawn male boxer with a good black mask.

German Shepherd Dog (Alsatian): A very popular dog and a well-trained Alsatian is a delight to know. He makes a good family dog and an able guard too. His coat needs regular grooming. Height: 24−26in (61−66cm).

Great Dane: Remarkable in size and very muscular. A fearless guard but with a charming temperament for his family. His short coat gives no problems. Height: 30in (76cm).

Hungarian Puli: A fairly recent addition to the Kennel Club Register. From Hungary, his coat hangs in tight cords which can go right down to the ground when mature. Height: 16−18in (41−46cm).

Mastiff: A very solid, heavy dog who usually has a very placid temperament. Short coat. Height: 30in (76cm).

Newfoundland: Very strong bone throughout. Lovely head with expressive eyes. A most docile, good-natured dog. Makes a devoted companion. Coat dense. Height: 28in (71cm).

Norwegian Buhund: One of the smaller dogs in this group. Kept as a farm dog in Norway. Coat is close and harsh but smooth. Height: 18in (45cm).

Old English Sheepdog: A very active dog that needs a good deal of exercise. His profuse coat needs very regular grooming. Makes a good companion. Height: 22in (56cm).

Pyrenean Mountain Dog: From the Pyrenees where he is used as a guard-dog. Should be gentle and docile. Has a profuse undercoat with longer outercoat and needs regular grooming. Height: 28in (71cm).

Rottweiler: A guard-dog and one of Germany's foremost working breeds. Naturally very bold. Coat is medium length. Height: 25−27in (63.5−68.5cm).

St Bernard: Known as the Good Samaritan Dog because St Bernards have rescued many people on the Alps. Very large, powerful dog with either a smooth coat or a rough coat. Height: the taller the better.

Samoyed: A very attractive dog that is active and graceful. His coat is dense and needs regular grooming. Height: 20−22in (51−56cm).

Shetland Sheepdog: A favourite with many, who comes from the Shetland Isles. Long coat, mane, and frill; needs regular grooming. Height: 14in (36cm).

Welsh Corgi Cardigan: From Wales, he has been of great help to Welsh farmers. His head is foxy in appearance, his coat short. Unlike his cousin the Pembroke, his tail is moderately long. Height: 12in (30cm).

Welsh Corgi (Pembroke): The more popular of the two Corgis. A low-set, sturdy dog with a short tail. Coat of medium length. A very active dog that needs exercise. Height: 9−12in (25−30cm).

For all these breeds I have given the height or the weight of the male, the females being slightly shorter or less heavy, except in the case of the Pekingese which weighs slightly more.

By giving you all these details about the various breeds I may have confused you even more, and perhaps you are now having difficulty in choosing between one or two breeds. If this is the case, I suggest you attend one of the many dog shows that take place most weekends. Details of the U.K. shows can be found in the two excellent dog weeklies *Dog World* and *Our Dogs* — or from the Kennel Club at 1 Clarges Street, London, W1Y 8AB (telephone 01-493 6651).

If you apply for a Schedule from the Secretary of a Dog Show this will contain details of the breeds that will be scheduled. The most important shows are called Championship Shows and at these you will not only see more popular breeds, but less popular ones too; hopefully the breed or breeds in which you are interested will be included.

Buying a Puppy

Having decided on your breed, the great moment now comes for you to choose your actual puppy. This must of course be purchased from a breeder. If possible visit one or two kennels, which will give you a better idea of what to expect of the puppies and, of course, give you a wider selection.

Breeders of dogs are very busy people and work single-handed so often these days, so please be sure to make an appointment, otherwise your unexpected arrival may not be appreciated. In larger kennels where there may be a kennel staff an appointment is not quite so necessary, but is nevertheless a courtesy that kennel owners do appreciate.

I strongly advise buying your puppy from a kennel or from a breeder because by doing this you can certainly see the dam and very probably the sire too. You can also see the surroundings in which the puppy has been brought up which can tell you a lot about the puppy's start in life. Kennels that are dirty and perhaps even smelly are definitely not the best place for your puppy to start his or her life. You can also tell from other inmates in the kennel if they are well cared for or not, all of which is very important if you want to ensure that your new puppy has had every chance in life, right from the beginning.

When you have decided on your breed, the next step is to find a breeder and no doubt you will wish this to be as near to your home as possible. There is no point in travelling two or three hundred miles when there is a good kennel only fifty miles away. You may even be lucky and find one nearer, but never be put off going to a breeder by someone who tells you there is a good litter just down the road. You will hope to have the pleasure of your dog for anything from ten years upwards so it is worth every effort on your part to get a fine, healthy, well-bred animal right from the start.

Where do you find the names and addresses of breeders? Look in the two excellent weekly dog papers — *Dog World* and *Our Dogs*. These can be purchased from any newsagent. There is also a book called *The Dog Directory* that lists names of kennels and their breeds.

Having tracked down a kennel or kennels, make the necessary appointment to see the puppies. It is useful to have decided, before you venture out to the kennels, whether you are searching for a dog or a bitch. This must be your own decision and it can save a lot of time for the kennel owner if you have made up your mind which sex you wish to purchase. It is surprising how many people have visited our own kennels with one thing in mind, and when they leave have not only changed their mind about the sex of the animal, but also about the breed. It is fatal for clients to arrive at kennels with unsettled minds, particularly if children accompany them, and want the first animal they see which so often is not for sale. This produces tears and all sorts of tantrums that could well have been avoided with a little thought. All puppies look lovely and it is most tempting, especially for children, just to want to possess the cuddliest they can find.

As I have already said, the conditions at the kennel will give you a very good idea about the upbringing of the puppies and this is most important. It is quite likely that you will see the puppies to make your choice before they are ready to leave the kennel. The normal procedure in this case is for the new owners to put down a deposit on the puppy so that the puppy is reserved for them until it is fully weaned.

It is unlikely at this stage that you will be allowed to handle the puppy. This is simply because the kennel owner wishes to protect the youngster from picking up any infection that you may carry. All safeguards must be taken at this age. These pups will not yet have been injected against the scourges of distemper, virus hepatitis, leptospirosis, etc., and I am sure that you would not want to be in any way responsible, although unwittingly, for passing this on to them. Puppies should have a natural immunity from their mother up to about eight weeks of age and most breeders, particularly if they are keeping a puppy or puppies as show prospects, will have these puppies given their full course of injections about 10/12 weeks of age.

Although not allowed to handle the puppy you can readily see if it is a strong, happy one with clear, bright eyes and no discharge from the nose. If in a large litter there is one puppy that tends to hang back from the others this does not necessarily mean that it is going to have a shy temperament. It has probably been bullied a little by its brothers and sisters and it is amazing how quickly it will come out of its shell when it is given individual attention in a home of its own. The puppy should be well covered with flesh and if a big breed in size when mature, it should have good strong bone. Never consider buying a puppy that is not fit to run about merrily by itself by the time it is four weeks old. There could be something drastically wrong with its conformation. The puppy's coat should be free from all scurf and foreign visitors, such as fleas, lice, etc. Its breath should smell sweet and its gums should be pink and healthy-looking. If you are at all unhappy about the condition of a puppy, then that puppy is not for you; it is far better to select another one or go on to another kennel.

If you wish to make absolutely sure that your new purchase is fit in every way, you can, of course, ask the breeder to have the puppy examined by a veterinary surgeon before you take delivery. If this is your wish it is your responsibility to pay for the veterinary certificate. All puppies sold overseas require such a certificate but it is rare for a certificate to be requested for puppies going to new homes in the U.K. You can normally tell from the conditions of the kennel, the bitch, and the puppies themselves whether or not your puppy will be healthy; if you have any doubts at all it is better to visit another breeder and be completely satisfied.

When you take delivery of your puppy you will of course be permitted to handle it and make sure that it is in every way healthy and what one would expect from a reliable breeder.

Before you leave the kennels with your puppy there are certain things that the breeder should make quite clear to you. First of all, a diet sheet should be given so that you can continue to feed the puppy as it has been done in the kennels. This diet sheet will normally take you to the end of the first year in the puppy's life; be advised to follow it carefully.

The breeder will also tell you about the worming of the puppy. Do not think that because a puppy has worms this must result from bad management on the part of the kennel owner. It is seldom, if ever, even with all the precautions in the world, that these pests are not encountered in puppies, but with the many good worm medicines now on the market they are soon eradicated. It is usual for a breeder to have wormed the puppies on at least two occasions before they go to their new homes. It is essential that worms are got rid of as soon as possible otherwise it hinders the proper growth of the puppy, apart from any irritation to the puppy itself. The signs of worms in a puppy are usually quite obvious. Firstly the breath of the puppy is rather stale and unhealthy; secondly the puppy tends to draw its bottom along the ground; and thirdly the puppy has spells of hiccups. If worms persist the coat will become staring and lose its gloss; if the condition persists the puppy can become quite ill. If you see any signs of worms when the puppy is in your charge then it is advisable to have professional treatment from your veterinary surgeon.

If your puppy is about 8/9 weeks of age it is unlikely that it will have been vaccinated. If it has, the breeder will give you a signed certificate from the veterinary surgeon. If not, it is up to you to have this done. I usually recommend that you give the puppy about a week to settle down in his new home and then have his injections attended to. On no account must you allow your puppy to mix with other dogs or cats until it has been safely immunized.

You will be given a signed pedigree by the breeder and a Kennel Club Transfer Form duly signed by the breeder if the puppy is registered at the Kennel Club. If not, you should be given a signed Registration Form so that you are in a position to register the puppy if you so wish. If perchance you are purchasing a show puppy it is absolutely essential that you should be given either of the above two Kennel Club forms so that you may register the puppy, for no unregistered dogs are permitted to be shown.

Now you have your puppy, all the many forms and instructions (some say it is worse than registering the birth of a child), and you are all set to bring up your puppy as a very respectable and much admired part of your household, and one we hope that will repay all your patience and love with untold devotion. Good luck to you all.

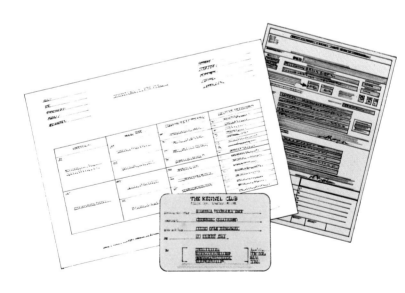

When purchasing a dog a registration certificate or partially completed registration form should be received from the previous owner.

Afghan puppies, four days old.

A smooth-haired dachshund with her litter.

The correct method of holding
a young puppy.

Boxer with pups.

First Days Away From Kennels

If your puppy was a little sick in the car going home this is nothing to worry about. Just remember that this change-over period from kennels to your home is a big step in the puppy's life, and that he needs your patience and loving care at this stage. When a puppy leaves all his friends and goes out into the big wide world there is so much that is new for him to absorb. Gone are the familiar kennel smells, even though they might have been only disinfectant. Gone are the familiar hands that cared for him and nursed him. Gone the companionship of his brothers and sisters, even though they did not always agree. Instead there are often loud noises that he does not understand, although many kennel owners today, in order to accustom the youngsters to noises, have radios playing in the kennels and I am convinced this helps them to accept noise when they come up against it in later life. It also seems to help kennel staff to get on with their work! He is introduced to children and even to the family cat; it is all very puzzling to begin with for your new puppy.

At this stage the diet sheet should be rigidly adhered to as any slight alteration could result in further upsetting for him. It is also wise at this early time for one person only to attend to him; to feed him and to look after his daily requirements. This makes the transition period easier for him, and easier for you, as he will more readily settle down to his new routine and future life. Animals on the whole are creatures of habit. When in kennels, his mealtimes would have been at a regular time, and this is another factor that it is most important to continue at the beginning of his new life.

If your puppy has not been injected against hardpad, distemper, etc. then, as already said, it is of the utmost importance that he is kept away from other dogs until he has received all his vaccinations. He should be strictly confined to your own garden until he is fully covered for the various virus diseases. If you do not have a garden then he should be confined to the house and taught to use a dirt-tray. Even if you think he is lonely and perhaps missing his brothers and sisters, do not be tempted to take him to tea with another of his kind simply to cheer him up. It may cheer him up temporarily, but at the same time he may well have picked up an infection that could be disastrous for him. I cannot stress this point too strongly. Be patient — far better to be safe than sorry. Give him a week at home and then contact your veterinary surgeon, who will give him his course of injections. This is usually done over a period of 14 days with two injections a fortnight apart. These two injections can cover distemper, virus hepatitis, leptospirosis canicola and leptospirosis ictero-haemorrhaiae. This should not upset the puppy in any way at all and it certainly does not hurt him. When he is fully injected then you can proudly show him to all your friends, both two-legged and four-legged.

The veterinary surgeon will give you a certificate giving details of the injections, which you must keep carefully in case at any time you have to put your dog into a boarding kennel. No reliable boarding kennels today will take an uninoculated dog. This is not only to safeguard themselves, but their clients' animals.

Your puppy should be given a little bed or box which he will know as his own, and there he should sleep both at night and during his daily rest periods. I think it is beneficial to bring up children alongside dogs — good for both of them as they must learn to respect each other. The children must learn to know that they must not overtire a puppy and that he must be left in peace to enjoy his rest period just as they did when very young. They must learn not to tease the dog, so spoiling his good temper, and they must learn generally to care for their companion in a proper manner. The dog must appreciate what belongs to him and what does not, and that there should be no sneaking off to pinch the children's toys, mother's gloves or father's slippers. He must learn that he has his own playthings, such as a ball or a rubber ring. The puppy must be taught where he is allowed to go and where he must not e.g. not on the best settee or in the children's bed. Bringing up a child or children with a dog can be a splendid way of teaching discipline to both parties and at the same time bringing not only benefit to them, but pleasure and joy.

Always ensure that there is a fresh bowl of water for the puppy to have a drink when he so wishes. This should be kept in the same place so that he will soon know where to go and get it.

Your puppy may feel a little lonely at night, and for the first two or three nights he may cry a little. Although it seems rather hard, do not give in to him. If you take him to bed with you, you will be making a martyr of yourself right from the beginning, for the puppy will not easily forgo this comfort. Most puppies have a decided mind of their own. This is part of their charm. If they think they can rule you they will not stop trying to do so even from an early age, and as they look so cute and appealing I know it will be difficult for you to resist. However, be quite firm, despite the family's criticism, and once your new charge realises that you mean exactly what you say he will adapt himself without further ado. Be assured that if your puppy has been properly fed during the day and is comfortable and warm at night, he needs no more attention.

In his early stages your puppy will require long periods of sleep so let him have as much as he wants. I am sure on occasions you will be quite glad when he does decide to have a little nap.

All dogs in the United Kingdom must have a licence, which is obtainable from the Post Office. This must be obtained when your puppy reaches the age of six months and should be renewed annually.

Be completely fair and firm with your puppy from an early age and you will be rewarded as he grows older and learns further general training.

Never leave your puppy too long on his own. This is the time when he will look around and see what sort of mischief he can get into. Try to plan so that when you have your puppy, for the first few months at least, he is not left alone for longer than just a few hours during the day. If necessary get a neighbour to look in and see that he is alright. If there is a real emergency and you have to go away for a complete day at a time, and if there is no kind neighbour to look after him, get in touch with your nearest boarding kennel. You can assure yourself of its reliability by checking that the registration with the local council, required by law, has been carried out. The majority of boarding-kennel owners also breed dogs and know how to look after puppies. If you have for some reason or other to leave your puppy for long periods, it is better that he is left in the care of someone who will give him the attention he needs. He will, of course, require to have his certificate from your veterinary surgeon saying that he has been injected against the various virus infections. Each year he should be given a booster injection and this will be noted by your veterinary surgeon on his inoculation certificate. This certificate is a most important part of your puppy's possessions.

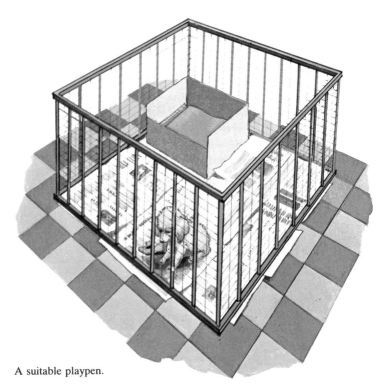

A suitable playpen.

Feeding, Exercising, and Housing

Feeding

Feeding is a very difficult subject to cover in such a small book. Every breed varies in the quantity of food that it should have. For instance, one would hardly expect an Irish Wolfhound to be satisfied with exactly the same amount as a Chihuahua. If one tried to feed a Cocker Spaniel or a Beagle on the same amount required for a Great Dane there would be disastrous results, as both the aforementioned breeds are usually greedy eaters and would do their best to live up to the amount required for a Dane.

Be guided by the diet sheet given to you by the breeder and stick to this as closely as possible. Very often you will find that the puppy, when away from his companions, lacks the incentive of competition to get what he can out of the feed bowl, and so does not eat as heartily as he might. The first feed that he usually wishes to discard is his milk feed, be it made with Farex, custard, porridge or some other cereal.

Normally at eight to ten weeks of age the puppy needs four meals a day — two meat-and-biscuit and two milk feeds. At three to four months he should be satisfied with three meals a day, again two meat-and-biscuit meals and one milk meal. At six months he is ready for two meals a day, with just a spot of milk at lunchtime. Gradually this milk feed can be done away with and he will be on two meals a day until he is about a year old. However, the number of meals required varies with the size of the dog and for such animals as the St Bernard, Newfoundland, Great Dane, Irish Wolfhound, which have to build up great bone, it may be that they need three meals a day until they are about 18 months of age. At all times be guided by your breeder's advice and diet sheet. Such people have had the experience of rearing many litters of the particular breed and know what they are talking about.

Fresh water should always be available for your dog. The water bowl should be changed every day and in hot weather several times a day. Unlike the water bowl the food bowl should never be left down so that your puppy can eat when he feels like it. This is a bad habit not to be

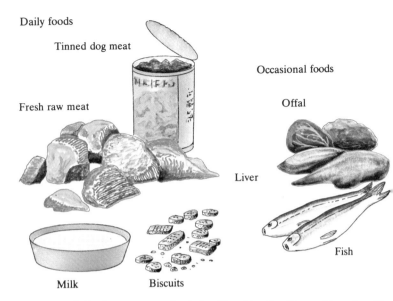

Daily foods

Tinned dog meat

Fresh raw meat

Occasional foods

Offal

Liver

Fish

Milk   Biscuits

encouraged. In the summer a dog's food bowl invites flies and insects with all their contamination and this can bring infection and disease. Give your puppy a reasonable time to eat his meal and if he starts to fiddle with it and be slightly uninterested, take it away from him and do not give him another opportunity to eat until he is due for another meal. He will soon learn that if he does not eat all his food it will be taken away.

On occasions fish may be substituted for meat to introduce variety and, of course, fish contains much-needed calcium and vitamin D.

To the convenience of the housewife, the excellent tinned food now on the market provides a good stable diet for your dog. This, with the addition of one of the good biscuit meals, makes life much simpler for the pet owner and is an adequate meal for any dog living the life of companion to a household. There are also dried meat meals on the market, and if your dog favours this type of food it is equally good for him, although I suggest that you give him something that looks a little more appetizing.

If your puppy is not getting enough of the right kind of food this will soon show in his coat and condition, in which case it is up to you to adjust his diet gradually.

Titbits and sweets should not generally be part of a dog's diet, but it is pleasant to give your dog a special little bit of something when he has been a good boy and responded to his training. There are many packets of such 'specials' on the market today and these, given in sensible proportions, can not only please your dog but do no harm to his overall diet.

A good hard biscuit for him to take to bed is not a bad thing either as it helps keep his teeth in good order and get rid of any tartar. It also helps the baby teeth to disappear and leave room for his new second teeth which are very important to the dog. The only type of bone that he should be given is a good old marrowbone from the butcher. This can either be cooked or fed raw. A dog should *never* be given any bones that are prone to splinter, such as chicken, rabbit or any other soft bone. A splintered bone can do great damage to a dog's intestines, just because owners do not consider the consequences of their actions.

Puppies must be allowed to rest after they have eaten. This is common sense as the weight of food places a great strain on a puppy's legs. If you want your puppy's legs to remain straight, as they should, keep him quiet after his meals.

It is perhaps interesting to note that in kennels we always feed raw meat, either tripe or beef, with a good biscuit-meal that has been soaked in gravy. In the winter we may add a little bone-meal or cod-liver oil to the mixture, but apart from that we have never given any other additional food. Puppies have eggs added to their milk once or twice a week, and bone-meal sprinkled over their food once a day. We believe very much in a natural food for the dogs and they repay us with lovely glossy coats, good bone, healthy constitutions, and happy, gay temperaments. What more could we ask?

Daily meat requirements for your dog

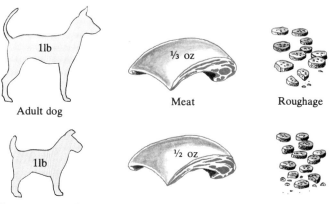

1lb

Adult dog

Meat

⅓ oz

Roughage

1lb

Puppy or young dog

½ oz

Exercising

Exercise for the family dog is of the utmost importance, the amount required depending, of course, on the dog. Kennel dogs are usually well catered for in this respect although recently, whilst judging, I have come to believe that not all show dogs are in the good, hard, muscular condition they should be. Good, free exercise is what a dog loves best of all and it is essential that he should have this sort of exercise to make him both mentally and physically fit. A dog should also have a certain amount of controlled exercise so that the muscles it does not use in galloping are used in the walk and trot.

A companion dog needs exercise to stop him getting bored at home from having nothing much to do, as well as to keep him in good health and condition. No matter how tempting it is for his owner to sit at home when rain beats hard on the window-pane, it is that owner's duty to see that his companion gets adequate exercise, particularly if he is a sporting dog who needs not only to stretch out his limbs but to tone up his muscles and air his lungs. Remember that you bought the dog knowing that such exercise would be necessary in all kinds of weather, and think what pleasure it gives you to see your dog enjoying his walks and thriving on them. Also, no doubt, the exercise will do you good too!

A puppy should not be over-exercised at any time and, as already said, never exercised immediately after his meals. As a youngster the puppy is better with two short walks a day rather than one long one. It depends on the breed how much exercise you give your puppy. The larger breeds, such as Danes and Wolfhounds, need no more exercise than they themselves want to take until they are about six months of age, and then they should be gradually introduced to their walks. For the toy breeds, they get more than enough exercise by just following their owners about the house and being free to lie down when they feel like it. You just have to use your common sense with regard to your own puppy and increase the exercise as he grows older; but never too much at any one time. This could cause irreparable damage.

Housing

I do not advise you to buy a brand new basket for a young puppy because he will take great delight in pulling it to pieces bit by bit. The same applies to those lovely cushion beds that fit around the dog as he lies down. These are luxuries that he can do without until he has got over his teething problems. Make sure his bed is draught-proof, but not too high off the floor to make it difficult for him to jump into. If it is difficult to teach your puppy to be house-clean, it is often advisable to buy a dog travelling-box from any of the good manufacturers on the market. He can

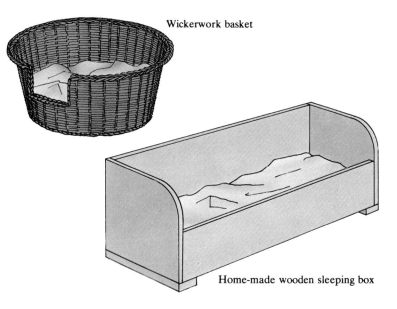

Wickerwork basket

Home-made wooden sleeping box

be shut in this box or cage at night. This often cures a dog that is difficult to house-train as most dogs intensely dislike making a mess in their own bed and will soon learn not to do it. (See General Training.) This cage or box has other advantages in that if for some reason or other you wish to shut your puppy away for a little while, he can be locked in his own box. He will soon know that this box belongs to him and will learn to go into it quite happily when he so wishes, as well as on other occasions when you put him there. Most medium-size show dogs of today who travel to shows in their own boxes will jump very willingly into them, ready to be on the way to the show. In this box your puppy can keep his own toys and play-things and it will be his refuge from humans or from other things. This box or cage can also be used in the car, where on occasions he may have to be left. Otherwise he might decide to have a good chew at the interior of your car. I remember once having all the electrics well and truly chewed in the back of our car when the car was only about two weeks old. This was done by a naughty beagle whom we should never have trusted, but he looked so innocent and I may say still does.

For the larger variety of canine it may be that you have decided that he or she must sleep outside. In fact it may be that you have bought the dog as a guard as well as a companion. Providing that you start with the dog as you wish to continue, there is no harm in keeping your dog outside. What

A fibreglass bed

is harmful is if you start with the dog inside and then discover that he is getting too big to be kept as a house-dog and for no other reason decide to move him to an outside kennel. This is detrimental to the dog and he will miss the companionship from being inside the home and will probably think that he has done something wrong. Think of this effect on the dog before you decide to take such action. If the dog is to be with you in the house during the day and then put outside at night, you must start this routine at the beginning; then he will not object to it. The kennel outside must be comfortable, clean, and completely draught-proof. Once again he will learn to recognize this as his own place and will become attached to it. If the dog will be in a heated house during the day (and this particularly applies in the winter), you must make doubly sure that his outside kennel is warm and snug. There is no need to heat it if the kennel is well insulated and a good big bed of straw or wood-wool is provided. This must be kept clean and he will snuggle down into this with great glee and make himself comfortable for the night. A dog must have sufficient space in his outside kennel to be able to stand up in it, and his bed should be of generous proportions and off the floor. Whilst most dogs curl up in a ball when sleeping, at the same time they, like us, enjoy a good stretch, so for this reason his bed should be large enough for this to be possible. If good clean straw is not available then invest in wood-wool, otherwise you will find your dog suffering from the effects of little mites and parasites that he has picked up from the straw. These little visitors can do untold damage to a dog's skin and coat in an incredibly short space of time, quite apart from the irritation and discomfort caused to the dog. In warmer weather a piece of carpeting on the bed or a blanket is quite adequate. These must be washed regularly and kept clean, otherwise they too can harbour fleas and other parasites.

For a dog housed outside it is a good idea to give him a run that surrounds his kennel. This means that if he has to be left alone he will be quite happy in his own quarters and, provided there is shade for a hot sunny day, he will be quite comfortable. By giving a dog a kennel and a run outside this does not reduce the amount of exercise that you must give your dog. He will look forward to his runs and change of scenery and in no way must he be neglected in this respect. The run can be made with chain-link fencing which should be concreted into the ground. The height of the fencing will depend on the height of your dog. This must be a safe haven for your dog and not somewhere from which he can escape if left unattended too long. The same applies to your garden: make sure that it is completely safe for your dog to wander round in, for if there is the smallest loophole, your dog will find it when he becomes bored and wants to search for pastures new. Never allow a bitch in season to be left alone in your garden. It is quite surprising where her admirers will come from and how they will get into the garden. If you cannot safely keep your bitch away from any followers when she is in season, it is far better to house her safely in a good boarding kennel. If perchance she is unfortunately caught by some ardent lover, then take her immediately to your veterinary surgeon, who will give her an injection to prevent her from having puppies. This does not mean that she will not be able to conceive to a dog of your choice when she next comes into season. The injection will bring her into full season again, so rather than be caught twice when she could not have a further injection, as this could be most injurious to her health, it is best to play safe and put her into the care of a boarding kennel. She may have to stay there for a period of three weeks but this is surely better than having wailing attendants on your doorstep with the risk of yet another mistake.

From one extreme we go to the other and think of the toy breeds. These can be marvellous little characters and in some ways they are more possessive than their bigger relations. They are usually rather sensitive to being shut away from their owner. Here again one of the many small carrying cages on the market can be useful. If you want a reprieve from your puppy running around under your feet, it can be popped into the cage and because it can still see you it is quite happy. Many of the toy breeds are Peter Pans and never seem to grow up. If they are taught to go into their box when you have things to do that you believe you can do better without their help, then they are not too upset if you put them into their box for a little while. What you train them in the early stages can be so important to them and to you in later years.

No matter where your dog is housed, outside or in, it is of the utmost importance that an ample supply of clean, fresh water is available.

An outdoor puppy pen should provide shelter and water

Grooming

The grooming of your dog is one of the most important aspects of caring for him and this should be done thoroughly every day for his good. Regular grooming contributes greatly to his cleanliness and to the health of his skin, helping to avoid any skin problems. If regularly groomed you will notice immediately when the dog has any parasites — before he takes the only course open to him, that is, to scratch himself and tear his coat and skin. Hair grooming also stimulates the sebaceous glands and thus provides oil to keep the hair in condition.

Dogs kept indoors in air-conditioned flats or houses tend to shed hair fairly constantly with a further increase at normal shedding times. Therefore to get rid of this dead coat it is absolutely necessary to have regular grooming. If dead coat is allowed to remain, particularly in long-coated dogs, it will cause great irritation to the dog and make him uncomfortable and even hot-tempered. With short-coated dogs it may just be possible to give your dog a good grooming every other day but, on the other hand, if trained from when a young puppy he will enjoy the attention of being groomed every day.

The amount of grooming required and the tools you will need for the job will depend on the breed you have acquired.

In this book I am dealing only with pet grooming or clipping, not with preparing the show dog. The basic difference is that in pet grooming clippers are used to trim the dog, while for show grooming the coat must be hand-stripped, which means that the hair is plucked out with the fingers or with the aid of a stripping knife. If clippers are used, particularly on any of the terrier breeds, the coat will lose the sort of coarse texture which is so essential for all terriers for the show ring.

For short-coated dogs all that is required is a good hard brush or rubber glove, dependent on coat texture. If the dog is groomed with one of these every day there should be no problems. For an extra polish on the coat, an ordinary shammy-leather can be used to finish off.

For dogs with a thicker coat a good wire pad with a handle attached is excellent. The wire teeth should neither be too harsh nor too soft, and set

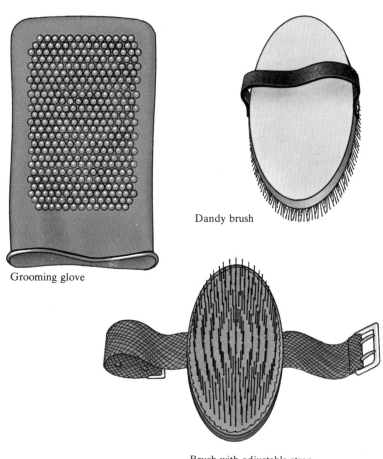

Grooming glove

Dandy brush

Brush with adjustable strap

Oval bristle brush

42

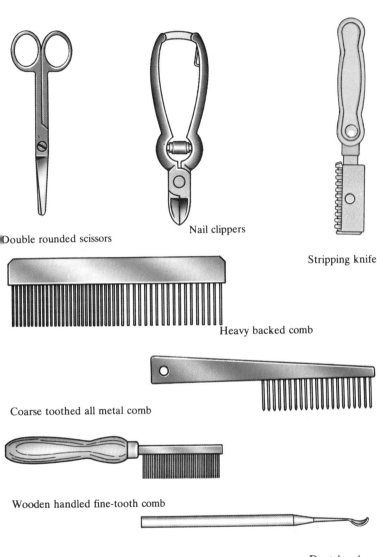

Double rounded scissors

Nail clippers

Stripping knife

Heavy backed comb

Coarse toothed all metal comb

Wooden handled fine-tooth comb

Dental scaler

These are some of the many useful items that can be
purchased for dog care and grooming.

into the pad with a foam backing (see diagram).

The best all-round comb is one with medium teeth on one side and fine on the other. To tease out the mats and tangles, use the medium side and then the fine side for the final combing of the coat. If the coat is badly matted or has foreign matter in it, then you must use a matting comb which is a heavy, coarse comb strong enough to bring out the mats or foreign material.

Never economize on scissors if they are necessary for your grooming kit. Buy the best you can, both for barbering and thinning the coat.

If you require clippers there are many excellent makes on the market which can be supplied by most good pet stores or bought at pet stands at dog shows. The standholders who have plenty of experience in the care of dogs' coats will be only too happy to advise on the best tools for your requirements. All necessary equipment, such as hair dryers, grooming tables, grooming post and loop etc. can also be obtained from the stand-holders at dog shows if you find difficulty in purchasing them from your local store.

Any thick-coated dog should not be bathed before he is brushed. This applies to Poodles, Old English Sheepdogs, Cocker Spaniels, etc. The coat should be completely free of all tangles and mats before it is put into water, as obviously a matted coat will become more matted once it is immersed in water and will be very difficult indeed to brush out.

In brushing out long-haired coats it is best to start at the dog's hind-quarters. This prevents the dog from actually seeing what is happening and he becomes accustomed to the brush and the friction of the brush. When brushing out the coat keep a hold of the dog's coat with the other hand and this will give him a certain amount of confidence. Never groom your dog on a slippery table. Try to put something under him so that he has a grip and can relax. Rubber mats are very useful for this purpose.

Begin by brushing one rear leg, first moving the brush up and then down in short, fast strokes, making sure that you get under the topcoat to the undercoat if he has one. Feel for any tangles or mats with your hand and comb these out first of all. From the rear legs advance to the front legs and then on to the bodycoat, working from back to front, not forgetting underneath the body as well. This is so often a neglected part. The importance of a very thorough brushing out of thick-coated dogs cannot be emphasized too strongly and only when this is done and the comb can run freely through the coat do you know for certain that you have done your job properly.

Bathing your dog — many have different ideas about when a dog should be bathed and how often. In my opinion a dog should be bathed when he requires it. It may be because he has rolled in something unpleasant and so carries a nasty smell which you can well do without. It may be that you have been a little lax in his grooming so his coat is not as clean as it should be. It could be also that he requires a medicated bath that has been prescribed by his veterinary surgeon. Whatever the reason, bath time can be a pleasant experience for both dog and handler.

Make absolutely sure that you have all your materials around the bath before you put your dog into it, for if you have to leave him for one second to fetch something you have forgotten, he will be unlikely to remain in the bath until you return. It is also a good idea to wear a rubber apron or protective clothing.

Make certain that the bath is of a size suitable for the dog and that it is quite steady. You will require a veterinary shampoo because ordinary human shampoos or soaps can be too strong for the dog's delicate skin. You will need a small human nail brush and a towel. Some prefer to plug the dog's ears gently with cotton wool to prevent water getting into them. This particularly applies if the dog has rather sensitive ears.

The water should be warm but not too hot and is best sprayed over the dog by means of a hose-pipe. The dog should be thoroughly soaked all over taking great care not to get any water, or worse still shampoo, in the dog's eyes. Once the dog has been completely soaked then the shampoo or soap can be rubbed into his coat, paying particular attention to see that his rectum is clean and tidy. With the brush get the lather over all parts of his body. When this has been successfully completed, rinse all traces of soap from his coat with the hose and make sure that his coat is quite clear of all soap before drying him. For this I prefer at all times to work on the dog from back to front. When you have rinsed him off in this way, squeeze all excess water from off his legs, tail, underparts of body, top of body, ears etc. Thereafter — and watch him carefully at this stage as he will delight in trying to jump out of his bath and give himself a jolly good shake — rub him briskly with a good rough towel before you dry him off with a dryer. If you have no access to a dryer, (and even an ordinary hand dryer will suffice for this job,) then you must give him an extra rub down with another towel.

If, of course, you can let him outside on a lovely sunny day to dry off naturally all to the good, but be careful that he does not choose the muckiest hole in the garden to roll in and get rid of excess water. His idea of being clean can be quite different from yours! Before the dog is completely dry it is as well to brush and train the coat the way you wish it to lie so as not to leave it to go its own way.

Excessive hair inside the ears should be plucked free. If this hair is rubbed with some hard chalk it causes the hair to become brittle and easier to pull out. This sort of chalk powder is available from any good pet shop. The hairs should be plucked with your finger and thumb with a quick motion and should only take a few minutes to do. Make sure that none of this powder is left in the ear. Never prod deep into the ear; just clean very gently with cotton wool as far as you can see. Make sure that the tips of your dog's ears are clean and not harbouring the remains of a meal. If your dog is constantly trying to scratch his ear or keeps shaking it, this indicates a matter for your veterinary surgeon.

Teeth should be watched as sometimes it is necessary to give help to remove the first teeth, particularly the eye teeth, when they are reluctant to let the second teeth take over. If they remain and the second teeth appear to be growing awkwardly, ask your veterinary surgeon to extract the offending baby teeth. As your dog gets older it may be that he will collect tartar around his teeth. This should be removed ('scaled') periodically and when necessary. If he has hard biscuits or a marrow bone to chew it is unlikely that he should be bothered with excessive tartar until his later years.

A good size marrow bone!

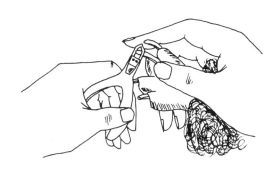

Clipping nails

Nails should be inspected occasionally. If your dog is regularly exercised on hard surfaces it is doubtful whether he will need any help in keeping his nails at the correct length. There are several types of nail-scissors available (see diagram), but I prefer the guillotine type because they are easy to use. If you have to use them, be careful not to cut the quick as this can be very painful to the dog.

Dew-claws on most breeds are removed when a puppy is three or four days old. If this has not been done keep a watchful eye on claws and cut as necessary. I have seen nasty dew-claws where the claw itself comes right round and digs into the dog's leg. They serve no useful purpose and in my opinion are best removed when the puppy is very young. A torn dew-claw can cause unnecessary pain and bleeds excessively. It was said in the past that dew-claws were retained so that the dog could keep his teeth clean with them. I think we have better methods today.

If you do find fleas or lice in your dog's coat there are many powders available today that can deal swiftly with these menaces. Take action immediately you find any of these parasites: the sooner they are eradicated the better (see diagrams).

General Training

A well-trained puppy is like a well-trained child: it gives great pleasure to many, it is pleasant to have around, it knows its place, and it does not rule the house or anybody in it. In fact, it is something that anybody concerned with can be very proud to own, and justifiably so. It can be the envy of many and a great reward for the patience and love that you have bestowed upon it to make it such an acceptable part of your life.

Not every puppy or dog can be so well-trained; there must be the odd bad one that never takes to discipline.

Having spent a reasonable time deciding on the breed and sex of your puppy, let us hope that you have bought a puppy that will respond to your training, patience, and care. If, however, you happened to take your puppy on second-hand, from somebody who was no longer able to keep it, or from the R.S.P.C.A., or another source, the animal should already have had at least some basic training. If this has been good and the animal sensibly handled then you are fortunate and need only continue the good work. If you have to battle with an already badly-trained dog there can be difficulties and heartbreaks in store for you. In these cases, extra patience is required and you should not blame the animal altogether.

Let us assume that you have acquired your puppy from a breeder at about the age of eight to ten weeks. You take him home where, of course, you are kind to him — but never forget that to be kind you must also be quite tough with his discipline and his training. A strict routine for the puppy is absolutely necessary and the most beneficial basis for any training. In doing this you can inspire your puppy with great confidence and at the same time by sympathetic and understanding with him. Do not overdo picking him up and fawning over him, fussing and cuddling him. It may be very tempting but it really does him no good in the end. He must grow up into a strong, healthy dog, well able to look after himself. If he gets too much of this sort of petting, as he matures he will not turn out to be the happy, gay, gentle-natured dog that you had imagined. Never forget that your puppy will only grow into what you make him.

When the puppy comes away from his kennel mates he is stepping into a world he has known nothing about. Everything is strange to him and for the more timid this can be a very frightening and worrying time. Even the bravest puppy will have some moments of apprehension. However, with considerate handling, patience and simple common sense he will recognize that he is among friends and soon settle down to be part of the household. As said before, at this stage it is very important that his diet should match as closely as possible the one that he was reared on. This is to avoid any stomach upset at this crucial stage of settling down to his new life.

The initial training or basic training of the puppy must consist of just three things — firstly, he must learn the words 'No' and 'Yes'; secondly he must learn his name; and thirdly, of course, he must learn to be clean in the house.

In training your puppy never confuse him by using a long string of words, and the words you do use must be spoken in the manner that you mean. For instance, it is no good saying 'No' to a puppy with a happy, breezy pronunciation. When you say 'No' that is what you mean and the tone of your voice must indicate that everytime the word is used. Contrariwise when he has been good and you want to tell him so, do it in a gentle, quiet voice with a little pat. He will soon know from the tone of your voice whether he has been good or bad and whether he has done right or wrong. Never, never torment your puppy or allow the children to tease him. This can considerably upset his initial training simply because you are making him muddled in his mind; he cannot understand, nor can he be expected to understand. If you are fair to him at all times he will understand this.

Having selected a name for your puppy use it every time you want the puppy to come to you or do something for you. He will soon realize that 'Patrick' or 'Victor' belongs to him. When you call him and he comes, do not forget to praise him and perhaps even give him a titbit so that he fully understands he has done well and pleased you. People often ask if dogs are easier to train than bitches. I do not think that it makes any difference which sex you have as far as training is concerned. I have had equal success with both females and males.

The great majority of dogs want to please their masters and find great pleasure in doing so. A well-trained dog is a happy dog and perhaps it is as well to remember this when sometimes you feel your training is not progressing as quickly as you had hoped.

At eight to ten weeks of age a puppy has really only three thoughts in his head. Firstly, of course, food — this is very important to the puppy. Secondly, he loves his fun and games and your companionship. Thirdly, having had enough of the first two, he must sleep. It is the combination of these three things that should be used to educate and train your new friend. His rest is just as important as his playtime and he needs frequent rest periods to help restore the physical and mental energy that he is continually using up.

Now to the important question of house-training. The sooner this is started the better, since bad habits can be learned very quickly and if they are not stopped at the beginning they are difficult to rectify quickly.

When puppies leave the breeders they are usually on three or four meals a day and, as already stated, this should be continued for a short while, until the puppy has settled down in his new home. After each of his meals and after his rest periods, when he is just beginning to stretch and wake up, he should be lifted gently and taken outside into the garden and given plenty of time to perform his natural functions. When he has done this, praise him and bring him straight back into the house. If this procedure is consistently carried out he will soon learn what is required of him and will begin to trot to the door himself. At this point he must be told he is a good dog and let outside to attend to his needs. You must give him your full co-operation at this stage, just as much as you need his, and if he goes to the door asking to be let out his request must be complied with immediately and not neglected simply because you are, for example, watching an exciting T.V. programme. This is a very important part of his training (I am sure you agree) and must *never* be neglected.

During the day this training should present no great problem and with patience and kindness the puppy will very soon learn what is required of him. Of course he is bound to make the odd mistake or two and must be scolded when he does so, provided you catch him in the act. It is no good punishing him if the deed has been done and gone unnoticed as this will only confuse him for, at this stage, it is unlikely that he will remember what he has done or even know what you are trying to scold him for. If you catch him in the act this is quite different and he must be made to realize that this behaviour is not good enough and will *not* be tolerated. Point to what he has done and say firmly to him 'No! No! No!' and then put him outside in the hope that he will finish off his business in the proper place. The old idea of rubbing the puppy's nose in the offending puddle has perhaps been proved effective, but there are many kinder ways of teaching good manners, more respectful to your puppy, that I certainly do not advocate this rather crude method. If he persists in being a naughty boy during the day and his toilet habits do not improve, it is a good idea to have a rolled-up newspaper handy for, in addition to admonishing him with your voice, a tap on his bottom with the newspaper can be very effective. It is not a good idea to smack him with your hands as a puppy can get the wrong idea about what hands should be used for and begins to think that they are there simply for the purpose of smacking him. This is an unfortunate association of ideas, as hands must be used for many more essential jobs in a puppy's life than just delivering a smack.

People blessed with gardens have a distinct advantage in the house-training of their pet as obviously they have the better facilities. But a puppy can learn to be house-trained in a flat or a home without a garden just as easily, although in a different way.

In the case of those who live in a flat, one would presume that the puppy would have his bed in the kitchen where, if he does soil the floor, it is not on the best carpet but on linoleum or tiles. Put some newspaper by his bed and encourage him to use this to be clean. I have had puppies that have trained to do this from six weeks of age and they rarely forget. Lift him out onto the paper and encouragingly persuade him to relieve himself. He will soon get the idea. Newspaper is also useful for the puppy during the long night when he cannot manage to keep his waste to himself until the morning. If he knows that he is permitted to use the paper in emergencies during the night he will be much happier, for once a puppy has been house-trained he loathes to make mistakes and can become upset about the whole matter.

Newspaper can be substituted by a box with sawdust in it or some of the special preparations that are now on the market for this purpose, mainly intended for cats. Once the puppy gets the idea of the newspaper or box, it can be removed to a place remote from his bed by gradually placing it a little further away each day until it rests where you want it to be. This method of house-training can also be used by people who have gardens. Here the method is that the newspaper is moved further away each day until it is placed outside the door. This usually works very well and in any case it is an admirable way of training a puppy during the winter months when he is still very young and a lengthy visit outside in filthy, cold, or wet weather could be damaging to his health.

Puppies are generally very intelligent about this aspect of their training and soon learn what is required of them. Some take a little longer than others but it is quite useless to become frustrated with a puppy and no good at all to lose your temper with him. Try to be patient at all times and have sympathy with the youngster, for only by having patience will you be rewarded. By becoming unnecessarily cross with the animal you will only tend to confuse him; at this stage of his training causing confusion in his mind will be fatal for progress.

There are, of course, some difficult cases and these can be both unpleasant and a nuisance, but even these dogs can be trained to be decent citizens. In such cases I have found that instead of giving the puppy a bed or a basket to sleep in, he should be given a box with a door that can be shut at night. He will be unlikely to dirty his own room.

A puppy should have his own toys so that there is no excuse for him to start chewing other people's possessions. If he is found guilty of doing this he must be told 'No' very firmly and the object taken away from him and one of his own possessions given to him instead. If he insists on returning to what does not belong to him, he must be scolded each time he does it and here the rolled-up paper can be very effective; not too hard a tap but enough to make him realize that you mean what you say. When he gets the hang of this and responds to your 'No' be sure to praise him and tell him he has been a good boy.

When the puppy arrives in his new home and he find that when the lights go out at night he is completely alone and in the dark, it is understandable that he might be unhappy and have a howling or barking session. Wait for a minute or two and see whether he is going to settle, or persist in crying. If he continues to scream, go back to him and check his bed and see that he is comfortable. If he appears to be a little restless pop him outside for a minute or two in case he wants to relieve himself. Having done this, speak to him kindly. Then the light must go out and he be left to his own devices. If he persists in making a noise, go back to him again and speak crossly to him, again using the words 'No! No! No!'. He should now realize that because he only gets spoken to harshly when he has been naughty, he must be doing something that is not at all approved of. He does not really want to displease you or upset you, so he must resign himself to the fact that he has to learn to be left alone in his own bed for the remainder of the night. As I said in my chapter on housing, do not let his appealing eyes convince you that you are being brutal and beastly to him. To feel sorry for the little chap and take him off to bed with you is a fatal mistake. You are making a rod for your own back and it will be twice as difficult to leave him the next night. Most puppies are anything but stupid and of course they will adore to curl up at the foot of the bed of their master and pretend they are little angels. Nothing could be more pleasing to any puppy that is allowed to get away with it.

The basic training of any puppy is highly important and because it must start at an early age it is advisable that the elementary training, such as I have described up to now, be given to the puppy before he has really established himself as part of the household. Such training will not tire him unduly as each little lesson will be of short duration. When he has mastered being clean in the house, to recognize his own name (the one you have been calling him since his arrival), and the meaning of 'Yes' and 'No', he will be well on his way to being capable of mastering the further training necessary to make him your well-behaved and devoted companion.

He is now ready to go further and be taught what collar and lead entail.

Some puppies take to these quite naturally but you occasionally come up against the stubborn pup who either behaves like a bucking bronco or digs his feet into the ground and refuses to move. This is often caused by leaving lead training a little late; a puppy should be taught this as early as possible after his arrival in his new home. A puppy that digs his heels in and firmly refuses to move is the most difficult to cope with and requires great patience. If you look at his face it usually shows tremendous determination with almost a hurt look which makes it difficult to refrain from smiling at him — you must not laugh or it will spoil the whole performance.

To get the puppy accustomed to a collar before attaching the lead to it, obtain a soft round collar and put it on once or twice each day for a brief period at a time when you are there to watch what he is trying to do about it. He may take no notice at all of this encumbrance and this is encouraging for you. If he does take notice, and seems to seriously object to it, take it off and when he is having a few moments of petting put the collar on again and give him confidence by talking to him, stroking his head and behind his ears, tickling his tummy etc. Under these circumstances he will soon forget that he is wearing a collar. A few lessons like this will soon dispel any dislikes he may have of the collar. Never lift your puppy onto your knee, or the chair, or settee when you are petting him. His place is firmly on the floor unless, of course, you do not object to him sprawling all over your furniture. This particularly applies if he is one of the larger breeds that grow up into quite big dogs. Bend down to him to pet him and make a fuss of him, but do not encourage him to climb onto your chairs. Just think how disastrous it would be if, after a good gallop in a wet garden, he were to dive into the house and decide that the best way to get dry is to jump onto the settee and roll about on it. If you have encouraged him to go on your chairs etc., you only have yourself to blame. The habit of climbing onto laps can easily lead to one of jumping up at people and this is certainly something to be avoided.

The collar should be removed whenever your puppy is running around his own home or garden. If it is left on, apart from making a slight mark on his neck while he is exploring his own home and garden, the collar could possibly catch on posts or trees. When the dog finds that he is unable to free himself he gets worried and agitated and with his twisting and struggling the collar could tighten, with disastrous results. Accidents such as this do easily happen and it is no good being wise after the event. We never leave collars on dogs in kennels and particularly not choke-chains, because they can do just exactly what their name implies. Choke-chains are excellent for training purposes as I will explain later. You should never use a choke-collar on a young puppy.

A long leather lead for training can be used with either a rolled leather collar or a check chain.

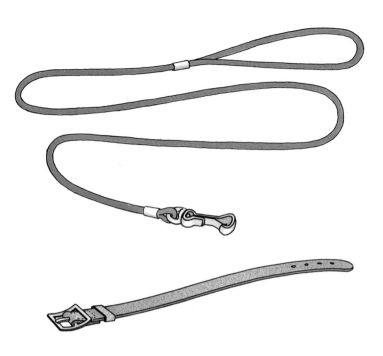

Lightweight lead and collar

Double slip collar

After about a week the puppy should have become so accustomed to the feel of the collar that the lead can be gently clipped on. Lead him firmly up and down, encouraging him all the time with kind words, and always praising him when he had done something to please. This exercise must never be treated as a game but a very serious part of his training. If it is done for one or two short periods each day you will soon have him walking reasonably well by your side.

To teach him to walk to heel on the lead, buy a slip-lead from your pet shop and place this over his head and, with your puppy on your left side, give the command 'Heel' and walk straight on. Having had the experience of the collar and lead for some days he should respond to the walk-to-heel exercise quite quickly. If he pulls away from you, jerk him back using the command 'Heel' or 'Heel' plus his name. The moment you feel he is alongside you, let the lead slacken and he will soon realize that if he runs on or lags behind he will get a nasty jerk in the neck. It is, of course, very tempting for him to pull away to investigate the many lovely smells that he finds on his travels, but he must keep this pleasure until he is sufficiently well trained to be let off the lead. In lieu of buying a slip-lead it is just as effective to use a choke-chain plus a lead. The choke-chain must be put on the right way, with the clip of the lead on to the end that will serve as a choke (see diagram).

Next we come to the 'Sit' exercise. This is a very important one in a young dog's life and absolutely necessary for successful discipline. This exercise can be taught as early as ten to twelve weeks, when the puppy should be able to recognize the word 'Sit' and eventually to obey.

The correct sitting position should be established from the word go, as nothing is worse than a dog lying half down and half up in a rather sloppy mess. The puppy should be taught to sit with his back quite straight, and his chest well out, and with an alert expression. Put on his collar and lead and take him to a quiet spot, preferably where he can sit with his back to a wall. Press your hands on his hips and at the same time tell him to 'Sit'. Keep pressing him down until he obeys your command and then praise him. Repeat this several times until your puppy understands just what you want. To begin with, do not continue these lessons for too long at a time when he will quickly get bored and want to dash off at the slightest opportunity to find something more exciting to do. If you have to be cross with him, do it only with your voice. He should by now know what a cross voice means. Here again you must only use the one word 'Sit', or this word with his name, but do not confuse him by saying 'Sit down' or any other additional words. At this stage of the puppy's training it is essential that he be taught by one person only, that only one member of the family should take part in his actual lessons and, of course, that only one person should speak to the puppy at any one time. Can you hear properly if two people speak to you at once? Of course not, so why should the puppy? I have seen, rather pathetically, several members of a family trying to convey something to a dog at the same time, with the result the dog does the only sensible thing and pays no attention to any of them and goes his own way. If you muddle your dog he will give up trying.

When he does obey, never forget to praise him. Perhaps on occasions or at the end of a lesson he can be given a much-looked-forward-to titbit as a reward — but not too many in case you overfeed him.

When you have got him to the stage that he will quite happily sit on command, take him away from his own surrounds and into a public place and make him put into practice what you have taught him at home. If your initial training has been correct this should not be a difficult operation and he should be perfectly happy to sit as told. Do not forget, however, that there will probably be many distractions in a public place, even to the extent of thoughtless humans who will want to come up and pat the dog. He must learn to ignore all these things and he certainly needs all of your understanding and sympathy for this lesson. At first it is not an easy lesson, but patience will be rewarded.

Teaching a puppy to sit
A puppy can be taught to 'sit' in this way. Holding the food bowl at mealtimes you can gently push the hindquarters down.

Having got this far take him back to his own training ground for the more advanced lesson of 'Sit-and-Come'. Attach some rope or stout string to the end of his lead and, having told him to 'Sit', back away from him slowly for about two or three yards. If he attempts to move shout 'Sit' in a firm voice, continually looking at him with steady eyes and concentrating on him. When you stop, call to him 'Come' and with your right hand signal for him to come, and with your left hand just a very gentle pull on the rope or string for his guidance; never tug him. Give him full praise when he obeys and he will be pleased that he has done what you wanted. Make him 'Sit' in front of you and he should look up to you with pleasure in his eyes. Repeat this once or twice — no more at this stage or he will get fed up with the whole procedure.

Next day lengthen the rope, and do likewise every day thereafter until you can successfully complete the exercise from quite a distance. If he has gained confidence in you, which he should have by now, you will be able to go on to the next step in which you slip the lead off and walk away from him, knowing that he will stay put. When you turn round call 'Come' and give the same indication as before with your right hand and your pupil should immediately come straight to you and sit in front of you. He will love this exercise but the success of it depends entirely on you. Although his progress can be a little slow, you must never be impatient with him or, worse still, lose your temper. If he loses faith in you it will need a great effort to restore it and you will find yourself back at the beginning of his training. This is most tiresome and disappointing for both dog and trainer.

You now come to the exciting lesson of 'Heel free'. Make him sit on your left side and then slip off his lead and with the word 'Heel', you both walk ahead. You can use your left hand to encourage him to follow by patting your own thigh, and if he wants to try and put his nose against your hand let him do so. This will give him confidence to stay with you. Also at this stage you must continually talk to him, encouraging him to come along. If he strays he must be commanded to come back to heel immediately and having done this, be praised for doing so. This exercise should naturally never be practised in a busy thoroughfare as until he is an experienced dog the slightest thing can detract his attention, tempting him to wander off and perhaps causing an accident. Keep this exercise for the open spaces and your own garden. Of course, it is a marvellous grounding for the dogs that go on to the show ring, the obedience ring, and for the much more advanced work of the police dogs and guide-dogs for the blind.

When near traffic, for obvious reasons, your dog should never leave your side. When you want to cross a road, tell your dog to 'Sit' and he should remain at your side until you have seen that the way is clear. You then command your dog to 'Heel' and off you go. When you have done this many times, albeit still on the lead, the dog will do this act instinctively without any commands from you.

Another habit that must be stopped right at the beginning is the natural one of your dog wishing to go and have a chat with other dogs. Apart from the possibility of him picking up an infection, he will not think about traffic and will bound off to meet one of his own sort with careless abandon, particularly if you happen to have a male and he scents a female in season. Teach him not to do this from a very early age, for his own safety and for your own satisfaction and peace of mind. He should on all occasions come to your command, if your teaching has been successful and, for example, if you let him off his lead in the country he should never think of chasing sheep, cattle or poultry. If he gives any indication of thinking about doing this he must be kept on his lead at all times, otherwise you will no doubt end up with a dead dog, an irate farmer, and being a very distressed owner. This is entirely your own responsibility and unless your puppy has had experience of these farm animals, at home or in his home surrounds, I would not recommend that you give him any opportunity to be free when such animals are about. He must have proved that he is absolutely safe with farm animals before he can be trusted with them. Much better to be safe than sorry.

A reluctant dog can be taught to 'come' with the use of a long lead

During all his training, never forget to allow him playtimes. For the pet dog retrieve-and-fetch can not only be a part of his training but also part of his playtime. This exercise can be started quite early and bring light relief to both the young puppy and the handler. Choose a soft article to begin with, when the puppy is about twelve weeks of age. He may show no inclination to take part in this exercise, in which case it is best to wait until he is disposed to join you. Gundogs are naturally more likely to accept this retrieving exercise but I have known other breeds that enjoy fetching and carrying.

Throw the article a little way away and tell your dog to 'Fetch it'. Usually he will trot off merrily and find his quarry. As soon as he reaches the article and picks it up, tell him to 'Fetch it' and encourage him all the time to come back to you. When he gets back give him lots of praise; when he releases the object give him something nice as a reward. The anticipation of this encourages him to let go of the article. When he does this well and enjoys doing it you can advance by making him bring back the object and sit in front of you until you take it away from his mouth. From there he can be taught to go round you and finish up sitting on your left-hand side. This all takes a great deal of time and patience so do not rush the youngster; it can lead to mastering the basic skills laid down by the many Obedience Training Societies. If you feel inclined to advance even further with your dog's training you will be made welcome if you join any of the recognized societies who specialize in Obedience Training. In the U.K. details of these can always be obtained from the Kennel Club at 1 Clarges Street, London, W1Y 8AB.

As you have bought your puppy to be part of your family he must learn to fit in with both the children and your domestic arrangements. Children must be allowed to play with him, but he must not be used as a toy. They must be taught to be kind to him, speak nicely to him, and use only the commands that you have taught him. They must never shout or scream at him, or tease him, or persist in lifting him up unless, of course, he has been accidentally hurt, in which case they should inform you straight away. As said before, the bringing up of a puppy and a child together can be a marvellous education for both and if done properly they will benefit from each other, learn from each other, and be loyal friends all their lives.

Once the puppy has settled in his new home and understands his basic commands there is no reason why the children should not teach him little exercises of their own, provided they do it in the same manner as you have taught the puppy and with the same patience. Some children have a marvellous understanding of animals which can be well and truly reciprocated by the animal.

A dog that barks just for the sake of it can be a perfect nuisance. This must be stopped as soon as it starts. He should be trained from a very early age that his job is to bark only at the arrival of strangers and that he should stop barking immediately he is told to do so, and when he can see that the strangers are acceptable to his owners. As you are likely to be present with him when this happens he should soon learn what is expected of him. What is more difficult to cure is if he insists on barking when he is alone in the house or alone in a room. The best way of dealing with this is to leave him in a room and when he starts to bark, creep back and scold him very severely with your voice saying 'No! No! No!'. If this has no affect and he repeats his barking performance then he must be chastised with a rolled-up paper which you should bang hard on your hand, again saying 'No' very firmly. He will probably look at you very sheepishly, wait for you to leave, and think about it all again. If he goes on barking go back and hit him over his bottom with the paper and again speak with a severe voice. He should soon learn that you are displeased with this habit, probably your neighbours too. If he is quiet for a period go in to him and tell him that you are pleased with him and perhaps even give him a titbit. There is nothing more irritating than a dog who constantly barks for no reason at all. There should be no barking except when strangers arrive. His training in this department must be consistent and successful, otherwise when you go out for the afternoon he will make a nuisance of himself and probably annoy your neighbours.

No dog should ever be allowed to bite unless he has good reason, e.g. an injury to himself that has made him not realize what he has done. If he starts to growl at the children or any of the family he must be chastised severely so that he knows he is in the wrong. There is only one answer for a dog that bites and that is for him to be put down — but with proper training this should never be necessary. If the dog has been badly teased by the children, one has to expect him to react as this is his way of showing his displeasure. Because nobody should tease their dog there should be no cause for him to become aggressive and bitter.

Chasing cars and bicycles is another nasty habit that must be stopped straight away. If your dog continues to do this, he must be kept on the lead at all times as, of course, he could cause a nasty accident by running after a car or someone on a bicycle. This is a habit that should never be allowed to start and it is only a bored dog who is likely to think of doing such a thing just to relieve the monotony. If he is well exercised and given all due care and attention he should not want to chase vehicles.

The rate at which the puppy's training progresses depends entirely upon your own patience and understanding of his limitations, on your insistence on fair play at all times, particularly where the children are concerned, and on your own common sense. Do not try to gallop ahead with his training if he is not ready, especially if he has not yet grasped what you are trying to teach him. See that he fully understands one exercise before you go on to another. Do not forget to buy a Licence at the Post Office for him when he is six months of age. It is also a good idea to provide a disc with his name and address on it to attach to his collar. His collar must be worn at all times when he is out on the roads and streets. This is required and enforced by Law.

Although there are many rules to follow, if you keep to the aforementioned simple code you should finish up with a happy, well-educated dog of which your whole family can be justifiably proud. However, if you do not end up with such a pleasurable companion do not blame the dog altogether. Stop and think where you might have gone wrong.

Reward of a titbit is appreciated

Showing the Family Dog

You have reared and trained your family pet well and are proud of him. Perhaps you have been stopped in the street by people wanting to admire your companion and have even been told that you should show him. Why not?

You have probably bought a book that tells you what your breed should look like. If not you can always apply to the Kennel Club for a Standard of your breed; this will go into all the details. You think your dog matches up very well to that Standard, so why not take him along to a dog show and see what the judge thinks?

Dog showing is a marvellous hobby and you meet many different people from all walks of life who have common interest in the dog.

All dogs entered at dog shows in the United Kingdom must be registered at the Kennel Club and you should have had the necessary papers to do this when you bought your puppy. If you did not register your puppy at that time it is never too late to do so, providing you kept the registration papers given to you by the breeder. With these you can apply to the Kennel Club for the registration of your dog.

The governing body for all dog shows in the United Kingdom is the Kennel Club and shows come under their jurisdiction.

Before you leap into the show world it is a good thing for you to go along to a show and have a look at what happens. Although at first it may look confused to you, when you understand what is happening it is simple and straightforward.

There are three types of shows — starting at the bottom with the Members' or Limited Shows; going up the scale we have the Open Shows; and at the top end there are the Championship Shows, where dogs can become champions. Great Britain however is the most difficult country in which to make a dog a champion as the competition is so fierce with the many thousands of good dogs that our breeders produce.

Schedules for any of the authorized shows are available from the Show Secretary. The names of these people can be found in the two weekly dog publications *Dog World* and *Our Dogs*. If you intend to show, it is worthwhile putting in a permanent order for one of these magazines as they do give you all necessary information about each show, e.g. venue, grade, and the Secretary's name and address.

The Kennel Club at 1 Clarges Street, London, W1Y 8AB, England will give you details of your nearest canine society. To start, contact the Secretary. In that way you can find out about your local activities. To make friends in the dog world you could then take part in their social functions. Dog matches are run by societies and these are usually held in the evening and are excellent training places for both new dogs and owners. As new people are continually coming into the dog world you will not be the only newcomer and you will be most welcome.

It is well for you to start at the bottom of the ladder and enter at a local Limited or Members' Show. These are often held on a Sunday or Saturday afternoon and make a very pleasant afternoon out for the family. At these shows you will get to know the procedure so that when you venture to the Open or Championship Shows you will already be familiar with what happens.

At the smaller shows you will perhaps find just one judging ring which will be surrounded by chairs or rope. At the larger events the dogs will be housed on benches where they remain except when they are being judged. At these events there might be up to forty rings. Most large all-breed Champion Shows, e.g. Cruft's, are run over two, three, and now four days. Up to 10,000 dogs might be competing at one of these shows and if it is a two day show this would mean about 5,000 dogs on show on one day — quite a sight and well worth a visit if you have never been to such an event.

Most laymen know about Cruft's and although Cruft's is the Kennel Club's own show (and a very important show to all exhibitors and breeders), it is not now the biggest show in this country as several of our General Championship Shows have more dogs entered. Cruft's is the show that most overseas visitors flock to, although even they are beginning to come to some of the General Championship Shows in the summer. A win at Cruft's means no more to an exhibitor than a win at any one of the other twenty-six General Championship Shows held throughout the year. All these shows award Kennel Club Challenge Certificates; to make a dog a Champion three of these must be won under three different judges and the dog must have won at least one of these Challenge Certificates after his first birthday. Whether these Challenge Certificates are won at Edinburgh, Birmingham, Belfast, Windsor or Cruft's makes no difference at all to the value of the Certificate.

There are also shows confined to one breed, which can be held in the same categories as mentioned earlier. Breed Club Championship Shows are always well supported and if you wish to see your own particular breed in force these are the shows to go to. For instance, shows for such breeds as Afghans, Irish Setters, Golden Retrievers or Alsatians, can muster no less than 500 exhibits of that breed including the top dogs of the breed in the country. It is a glorious sight to see top dogs all beautifully presented and hoping for top honours. If you really want to see your own breed in all its glory these are the shows to go to and you will find details in the dog papers.

If judging is advertised as starting at 10 a.m. it will start at that time. With the huge entries that dog shows have today there is never any time to waste. The judge will arrive in the ring in good time, usually accompanied by two stewards who give the exhibitors their ring numbers and generally assemble both dogs and exhibitors. On completion of this task the stewards retire to the judging table and leave the judge in peace to get on with his or her job.

What is the judge looking for? This question is sometimes difficult to answer, but generally he or she is looking for a well-constructed animal of the type as laid down in the Kennel Club Standards and with, if possible, that extra quality that turns a good animal into an even better one. A judge should know inside out the Standard of the breed that is being judged and it is his or her duty to give an absolutely impartial opinion on the dog. This happens in most cases, but it can sometimes happen that a little bias is shown for one reason or another. Such biased opinions do not go unnoticed and it is the exhibitor's responsibility to remember them and therefore not to show under that particular judge again.

Each judge that judges at a Championship Show requires the approval of the Kennel Club and to become a judge at this level requires many years of training and experience. Judges who have qualified to judge in more breeds than just a handful are termed 'allrounders'. They have a vast experience of many breeds and of judging in many countries throughout the world. Top allrounders, both men and women, lead busy lives travelling around the globe and can be booked many years in advance to judge one breed or another.

Exhibitors travel many thousands of miles during the year, at no small cost, simply to show their dogs; and as the great majority of exhibitors are also dog breeders, these are the people who keep dog shows going. For a dog society cannot thrive unless the entries at its shows are paying entries. It is always a high number of entries that makes a profit but it is always the exhibitor's prerogative to decide whether he will exhibit at a particular show or not. The decisive factor is often the judge. For instance, if a judge is known to have rather heavy hands with a dog, experienced exhibitors will not risk taking out their hopeful new puppies under that judge. For it is important that a puppy attending a show for the first time should be handled considerately and kindly. If a puppy is put off by rather rough handling it can take that puppy a long time to regain his confidence. There are, of course, other factors that will cause an exhibitor not to show under a particular judge, or at a particular show.

As so many shows today do not award prizes in money, dog-showing is becoming an expensive pastime. Consider the cost of U.K. entries: Championship Shows from £3 to £4 upwards per entry per dog;   Open Shows at about £1 per entry per dog;   add the cost of getting to the show, food, etc.;   it all mounts up. Bearing this in mind, it is surprising that entries at shows continue to increase and have reached a staggering proportion, which gives many show organizers problems fitting all the exhibits into the space available. This seems to be the case all over the world where entries for shows are in most cases much more expensive than they are in the United Kingdom. One can only conclude that it is the glory of winning that matters to exhibitors and the joy of seeing their stock do well in the face of terrific competition. Of course good wins enhance the value of animals and there is always overseas demand for stock from the United Kingdom.

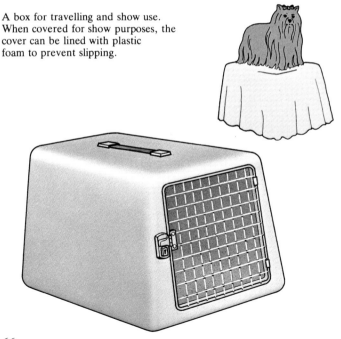

A box for travelling and show use. When covered for show purposes, the cover can be lined with plastic foam to prevent slipping.

Benching chain

Transportation cage

Table

"New" dogs (unseen by Judge)

Handler
Dog being examined by Judge

Judge

"Old" dogs (already seen by Judge in a previous class)

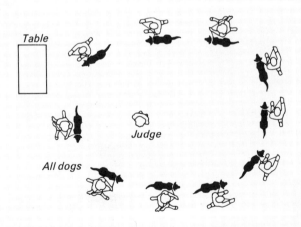

Table

Judge

All dogs

"Once round, please"

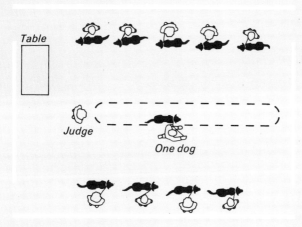

"Once up and down, please"

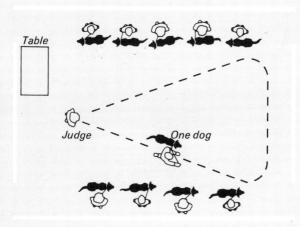

"Triangle, please"

A typical section of show benching

Ailments, Injuries, and their Treatment

Given reasonable care and attention dogs are generally healthy animals. If cared for along the lines suggested in the foregoing chapters they should enjoy perfect health for the best part of their lives.

Once you have acquired a puppy you should make contact with a really good, reliable veterinary surgeon, and preferably one who specializes in dogs or has a small animals practice. If you need advice, try one or two of your local breeders, for no matter what breed they specialize in they should be able to guide you on this important matter. Having found and introduced yourself to a veterinary surgeon do not bother him unduly, only when the need is particularly urgent. For instance, he will not appreciate being called out in the middle of the night only to discover that your animal has been sick and ailing for some days. In this as in all matters use your common sense. If you have a bitch in whelp it is well to let your veterinary surgeon know the date she is due to whelp. Then if you have to arouse him at an unreasonable hour he will not be surprised.

A dog's temperature should be in the region of 38.5°C or 101.5°F. Individual animals can vary slightly from this but if your dog appears off colour, e.g. not eating his food, listless and lethargic, irritable, or has diarrhoea, or a discharge from his eyes or nose, take his temperature immediately. If it is either up or down by a degree or two it is usually sensible to call your veterinary surgeon.

A dog's temperature should be taken with a blunt-ended clinical thermometer, the end of which should first of all be smeared with vaseline. Shake the thermometer to make sure that it registers a low reading before you take the animal's temperature, otherwise you could get a false result which would raise an alarm, causing unnecessary trouble. The thermometer should be held in place for at least the time stated on it and should have half its length in the rectum. Never ever force or push the thermometer into the rectum. A gentle pressure on the anus by the thermometer will relax the dog's muscles and allow it to slip in quite comfortably. When you have left it in long enough, withdraw it and hold it horizontally, twisting it round until the reading is quite clear.

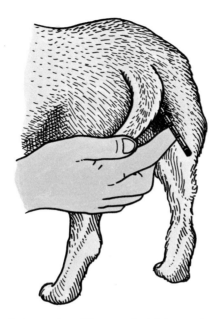

Taking a dog's temperature. The normal adult temperature of a dog is 101.5°F

Applying ointment to the eye

When the thermometer has served its purpose it should be cleaned by wiping it with a piece of cotton-wool that has been soaked in surgical spirit, and then replaced in its container ready for the next time.

On many occasions a low temperature can give more cause for worry than a high one, so do not think that all is well if the temperature is below normal. When nursing a sick animal it is important that the veterinary surgeon's instructions are completely followed.

When ill, your dog must be kept spotlessly clean, warm and quiet, and given his treatment with understanding and great patience. In order to give him a dose of medicine get him to stand or sit in front of you and if possible have someone to help you keep the dog steady. With the fingers of your left hand pull down the right-hand corner of his bottom lip and then gently pour the medicine into his mouth. Never open his mouth and attempt to throw the liquid into his throat. Apart from being nasty and uncomfortable for him, it could easily make him choke and be sick. A similar method should be employed when he has to take a pill. Gently open his mouth, speaking to him all the time, and then quickly put the pill on the back of his tongue and shut his mouth immediately. Keep his head held high and gently stroke his throat. When he swallows, the pill should go down. Then praise him again and give him confidence.

administering medicine

Accidents

If your dog is unfortunate enough to have an accident, is perhaps even run over, keep him absolutely quiet moving him as little as possible and get veterinary treatment straight away. Note that it is most unwise to give such stimulants as brandy where there is an internal or external haemorrhage. If your dog has cut his foot or leg badly, due to a road accident or on a bit of glass, bandage the wound as tightly as possible to stop bleeding and apply a tourniquet somewhere between the wound and the heart. To tighten the tourniquet push a pencil or something similar through the bandage and twist it. At this stage the dog will be under great stress and could quite easily and quite unintentionally try to bite. To avoid this, tape his mouth with a bandage or even an old silk stocking, before attempting to treat him. To tape the dog it is necessary to put the tape round his mouth a couple of times and then bring it under his throat, cross it, and bring it up on to his neck where you tie it very firmly. A tourniquet should not be left on longer than fifteen minutes at any one time.

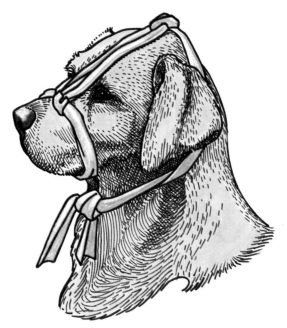

An 'emergency' muzzle

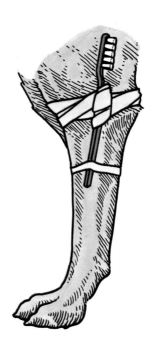

An 'emergency' tourniquet should be applied on a pressure point above the cut

For minor accidents such as abrasions or slight cuts, clean the wound and dry it with cotton-wool and then smear zinc or calamine ointment over it. Better still, of course, is penicillin ointment, but this is only available on prescription. If bandages have to be used, a restrictive measure will usually have to be taken to prevent a dog from tearing them off. Take a plastic bucket that has had the bottom taken out of it. Make holes round the bottom of the bucket and by threading string through these holes and on to the dog's leather collar the bucket should become quite safely attached to the collar. Pass the bucket over the dog's head and fasten the collar on him. With its head in the bucket the dog cannot get to its wound and although this may look rather uncomfortable, and no doubt is, it does allow the wound to heal quickly and without any interference from the dog. This is certainly a better method than muzzling the dog, because with a muzzle he will try and rub the wound and can make a nasty mess of it.

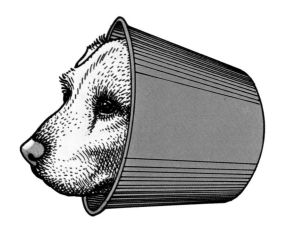

A plastic bucket adapted to prevent a dog from irritating a wound

Anal Glands

With a correct diet and where the motions are solid it is unlikely that these glands will give any trouble. If they become infected they can be a nuisance to the dog and cause great discomfort. The symptoms of trouble are easily recognizable. The dog will keep turning round to lick his bottom and will drag himself along the floor in an effort to relieve the irritation. The dog will even carry his tail covering his anus as though something was annoying it. A slight discharge and a foul smell indicate badly infected glands. So take the dog along to your veterinary surgeon so that he can squeeze the glands and rid them of their contents. If you wish to do this yourself take a fairly large piece of cotton-wool in your right hand and hold the dog by his tail or back-end with your left hand. Put the cotton-wool over the offending glands and gently press inwards and then upwards with your thumb and forefinger. This action should get rid of the matter from the glands. If the condition does not improve, take your dog to your veterinary surgeon for his advice. If the condition is allowed to persist it could easily turn into a nasty abscess.

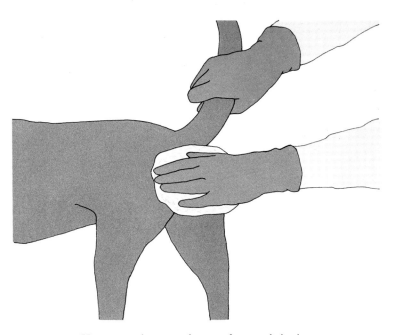

How to expel unwanted matter from anal glands

Arthritis
This is a disease involving a joint or the inflammation of a joint. It is usually confined to older dogs and can make the dog quite lame. Rest and warmth are essential, and soothing remedies can be applied.

Bites
If your dog is bitten by another animal, cleanse the wound and apply penicillin ointment or tincture of iodine until all the discharge stops. If it is a nasty wound it is better to have it treated by your veterinary surgeon who will probably give your dog an injection to prevent or halt any infection.

Burns and Scalds
Any dog living in a house runs the risk of being burned or scalded. If the burn is serious do not delay in calling your veterinary surgeon. Shock follows very quickly. The dog should be kept warm and quiet. It is a good idea to wrap him up in a blanket with hot water bottles if necessary. To treat a minor burn, gently clean the burn removing any foreign matter such as straw or dirt, and then as quickly as possible exclude all air from it

by applying olive oil or any oily substance. Cover this with dry gauze, cotton-wool and a loose bandage. It may also be necessary to put a hood on the dog to keep him from licking it. Most households now keep in their kitchen lotions to apply in the case of a first degree burn to a human; the same lotions can be applied to a dog when the burn is a simple one.

Canker

This is more common in long-eared breeds and is caused by tiny parasites getting into the canal of the ear and multiplying rapidly. They cause great discomfort to the dog and the condition should be attended to at once. It is best to take your dog to the veterinary surgeon immediately so he can tell you just exactly how to treat the dog. He can also show you how to apply his prescribed treatment. Ears should always be treated with great care as they are very tender and by poking down into them you can do more damage than good.

If you notice that your dog is scratching round his ears and you consequently find a dark, nasty-smelling substance in the ear or ears, you can be sure that your dog has canker. Of this there are two forms — wet and dry. Both need immediate treatment. If this condition is allowed to persist and becomes chronic only an operation, an aural resection, will sort the matter out. Although this puts the dog to great discomfort for a limited period, it is almost always a success.

Colic

This is a pain in the abdomen and is generally caused by indigestion, flatulence or constipation. It is mainly found in the larger breeds and is thought by many to be caused by incorrect feeding. Symptoms usually appear after a heavy meal when the dog begins to swell up and is obviously in great discomfort. If this happens, treatment must be sought immediately. Only prompt action by your veterinary surgeon can save the dog. Until you get treatment by your veterinary surgeon a piece of common washing soda about the size of a walnut will make the dog vomit and so relieve the tension on his stomach.

The cause of this ailment is unknown, but three simple precautions can be taken to help to avoid it: never give your dog heavy meals late at night; never feed him with unsoaked biscuit meal; and never feed him with food that is too wet.

Constipation

Once again the cause of this trouble is usually a badly balanced diet. The dog finds it difficult to pass his stools, which are generally very dry and hard. If this condition persists a change of diet should be tried and you should ask yourself whether your dog is getting enough exercise. If a change of diet does not sort the problem out then a laxative should be given. This can be liquid paraffin, Milk of Magnesia or Epsom Salts, in small doses over a period of time.

Coprophagy
Dogs occasionally suffer from this complaint, which means that they are eating their own faeces. The suggested cures for this unfortunate habit are many and varied. Some say the cause of the trouble is a vitamin deficiency, others say that it is an iron deficiency. In my opinion the best cure is to ensure that faeces are not left lying around to give the dog the opportunity of eating them. It must be remembered that most dogs will also devour the faeces of cows and horses if given the chance.

Corns
These are usually found on members of the big breeds with no long coats to protect their skins. They generally appear on the elbows and the hocks but can be prevented by ensuring that your dog has a comfortable bed and that he does not lie around on hard floor or concrete. Elbows and hocks can also be rubbed with surgical spirit to harden the skin and so help prevent ugly corns.

Dandruff
This is a scurfy condition of the coat and can be improved if regular grooming takes place. This will increase the circulation to the skin and stimulate its nerve supply. I feel that this condition too can be ascribed to a bad diet and lack of exercise.

Diarrhoea
In puppies this can be the result of worms, but it can also be caused by change of diet and improper feeding. If worms are suspected you must ascertain whether they are of the round or tape variety as they require different remedies. There are many perfectly safe preparations on the market than can be used to eradicate these pests. They must be got rid of to ensure the steady growth of your puppy. If the above-mentioned problems are not the cause of the diarrhoea and if it persists, a veterinary surgeon's opinion should be sought. Diarrhoea can also easily be the beginning of another more serious ailment, such as distemper or hardpad.

Distemper
Canine distemper is due to a virus that invades the nervous system and,

therefore, symptoms such as fits, chorea and even paralysis may arise and are seldom curable. It is a highly contagious disease. No owner should fail to have his dog given the inoculations. It will cause the dog to have a very high temperature and appear listless. He can also develop a cough and have a discharge from the nose; his eyes will look weak and sensitive to light. On no account should you take an affected dog to the veterinary surgeon's surgery; this will spread the infection. Your veterinary surgeon should be asked to call on your dog.

Nursing plays a great part in the dog's full recovery and needs great patience and skill as so often there are nasty side-effects. Much better to play safe and see that you have your puppy injected when he is about 8 to 12 weeks of age.

Ears
Canker has already been described and is often used by the layman as a description for anything that affects the ear. Sore ears are usually the result of carelessness as ulceration, which is seen as sores that are discharging pus, does not just happen overnight. Check ears at least once a week for any problems and stop them before they catch hold.

Entropion
This is much more common in some breeds than in others. Inverted eye-lids should be looked for in puppies that have rather weepy eyes and if examined more closely you will usually find that the lids are curled inwards in such a way that the lashes are irritating the eyeball itself. This condition appears to be hereditary and only an operation can put the matter right.

External Parasites
Any dog is liable to pick up fleas, lice or ticks, particularly if he is allowed free-range exercise in fields or woods. Many brands of louse powder are available today, so if you find these pests on your dog they can soon be eradicated. To do this successfully, not only the dog must be carefully treated but also his bedding and other habitual places of rest. Instructions are usually given on the packets; they should be followed carefully. Fleas can be persistent and will remain on the dog's bed for many weeks unless treated with dusting powder. Fleas and lice can cause skin troubles and general disability. The sooner you get rid of them, the better.

Eyes
The eye is a very delicate organ and when giving any treatment to it, care must be taken at all times to handle gently and not to exert any pressure

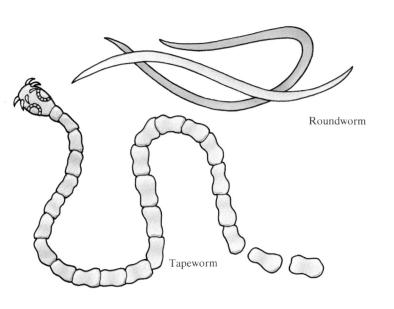
Roundworm

Tapeworm

Adult flea

Biting louse

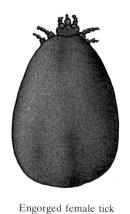
Engorged female tick

Mite (microscopic)

Sucking louse

on it. A slight discharge may be caused by a draught or a slight cold and this should be wiped off with cotton-wool or a tissue and the eye bathed with cotton-wool dipped in lukewarm boracic acid solution. If, of course, the eye does not improve and the discharge continues then this could be a symptom of a more serious disease and veterinary attention must be given to it. If a foreign body gets into the eye, (grass seeds have a bad habit of doing this in the season) then bathe the eye gently with the above solution and try to get the offending particle removed. These are often the cause of a swollen and rather red-looking eye. On no account should a dog ever be allowed to hang his head out of the car window. This is just asking for trouble and eye colds with serious consequences can be the result. If your dog happens to be unfortunate enough to get an acid of some sort in his eyes, immediately make a purse of the eyelids and pour in some castor oil or glycerine.

Feet
Split pads and eczema cause a dog to nibble at his feet and this often results in lameness. Gentian violet, now supplied in spray form, should be applied, although it will take time for the sores to heal properly. Cysts between toes can greatly annoy a dog; it is quicker in the long run to get rid of them by veterinary treatment. Toe-nails can be torn by a dog catching them on wire or tough grass etc. and can be very painful. For treatment, soak the paw in a warm antiseptic solution as often as possible and try to keep it clean.

If your dog happens to pick up some tar on his feet during the hot weather this can cause him great discomfort. The hair should be cut away from between the toes and a substantial amount of fat, lard or margarine rubbed well into his toes to soften the tar. Thereafter the feet can be thoroughly washed.

Fits
There are many different types of fits; some can be caused by a virus infection. It is best to consult your veterinary surgeon to find out cause and treatment.

Haematoma
This blood-serum blister is usually a side-effect caused by a dog scratching himself for some reason. It can also be caused by a blow. Unlike an abscess, such a swelling is soft at first and only later does a hard edge form. Haematomatas are most common on the ears of the dog. If they do not clear then surgical treatment is required.

Hardpad Disease

Canine encephalitis is caused by a virus and usually attacks the central nervous system. If an animal survives he is left with a thickening and hardening of the skin and sometimes the nose — hence the name 'Hardpad'. The symptoms are similar to those of distemper and like distemper prevention by inoculation is very much better than cure.

Hiccough

Although this is not a serious complaint it distresses the dog while it lasts. It is usually caused by indigestion but can also be caused by worms. Bicarbonate of soda in milk usually brings some relief.

Hip Displasia

This is a subject that is frequently discussed today and whilst some breeds seem to be free from it many are not. I think that this deformity is very difficult to diagnose. I have seen many dogs with a bad gait that some would say have hip displasia but when X-rayed they are found to be free. On the other hand, I have known dogs that have moved extremely accurately but whose X-ray shows them to have this malformation of the hip joint. Dogs with hip displasia can live to a great age and they can be just as active as dogs who have correct hips. Hip displasia is no serious impediment for a family pet that is not to be bred from.

Kennel Cough

This has in recent years become more widespread and seems to be contagious. Fortunately its effects on most dogs are not serious. It can be a problem in large kennels because it quickly passes from one dog to another. If young puppies catch the virus it can take a great toll on their general health. Adult dogs do not seem to worry much about it and, provided they are in good condition, usually manage to throw off the virus quite quickly. Treatment, if necessary, can consist of a mild expectorant with codeine and perhaps an anti-histamine. As this disease has proved to be so contagious, dogs suffering from it should be isolated and certainly never taken to shows or other places where they can meet dogs. Anti-biotics can be given by a veterinary surgeon to prevent secondary infections.

Leptospirosis

There are two forms of this nasty disease:

Leptospiral Jaundice: This disease is caused by food fouled by virus-carrying rats. The symptoms are fever, diarrhoea and listlessness with bleeding gums and sometimes a bleeding nose. The actual jaundice, as in humans, does not become apparent until a later date. An inoculation is available to prevent this disease and can be given at the same time as the distemper and hardpad injections. If a dog catches leptospiral jaundice no time must be lost in getting veterinary help.

Leptospiral Nephritis: This disease, like the jaundice, is a deadly disease that attacks the tissues of the kidneys. Again, an injection is the best safeguard against your dog catching this infection. Symptoms of the disease are a high temperature, lethargy, and loss of appetite. An affected dog roaches his back and loin and obviously has a certain amount of pain or discomfort from his kidneys. Often the dog has difficulty in passing urine and has an excessive thirst and foul breath. Call your veterinary surgeon immediately you notice any* symptoms, but again prevention is better than cure.

Metritis
This usually occurs just after a bitch has whelped her litter and is caused by the retention of membranes and afterbirth. This can soon be rectified by the veterinary surgeon, who will administer an injection of pituitrin followed by a course of another drug to clear up any internal infection.

Nettlerash
This is not serious but can be rather disturbing if you have not seen its effects before. The dog's head swells, lumps appear all over his body, and he looks rather pathetic. Fortunately it does not affect his appetite or general well-being. Usually it is caused by an allergy of some sort. *Urticaria* usually subsides on its own within a short space of time and requires no treatment.

Poisoning
You must act with great speed to get rid of any poison swallowed by a dog. Try to make the dog sick by giving him a piece of washing soda or just salt and water.

Rheumatism
Like humans, dogs can be subject to this complaint and can suffer severe pain if it is a bad attack. Aspirins administered to the dog three or four times a day soon put an end to his discomfort and effect a cure.

Rickets
This is usually the outcome of malnutrition. Again, prevention is much

better than cure. The term 'rickets' implies that the bones of a puppy have not formed correctly. This is due to bad rearing of either the puppy or his dam. The indications are crooked, knobbly joints, bowed legs, and a generally malformed appearance. In advanced stages the bones become soft and are easily broken.

Shock
This can set in after any severe injury. Keep the dog as warm and as quiet as possible. Never try to persuade a dog that is not fully conscious to swallow any liquid, but if he can take some liquid by himself, without any choking, then a drop of brandy or whisky in water can be both helpful and soothing.

Skin Conditions
A layman is prone to label any skin condition 'mange'. A correct diagnosis must be made by the veterinary surgeon who will take a skin scraping. Most skin troubles can be prevented and are usually due to the neglect of simple precautions. With so many preparations on the market today to help you keep a dog's coat in excellent condition there is no excuse for the dog to suffer from a skin condition.

Sarcoptic Mange: This contagious ailment, caused by a small parasite, can be easily transmitted by means of grooming tools, bedding, kennels etc. It usually starts by attacking the skin around the eyes, the outside of the ears, the elbows, and on the abdomen. Small red spots, looking just like flea bites, appear and the acrid matter they excrete sets up intense irritation causing the dog to scratch and bite himself. Sores and bare patches appear and the dog suffers great discomfort. It is readily cured with modern drugs such as tetmosol and benzyl benzoate.

Follicular Mange: This type of mange generally begins with a single, bare patch of dirty, greyish colour. Unlike sarcoptic mange, little or no irritation is caused, even though this is similarly a parasitic condition. This particular parasite looks like a small maggot. Some think that this skin condition is not contagious but congenital, i.e. passed on from family to family. Follicular mange is much more difficult to cure than sarcoptic and veterinary help must be sought.

Eczema: This is a non-contagious skin disease that many believe to be dietary in cause. I firmly believe that it is also a nervous condition. I remember an old bulldog coming in to board one afternoon and by the evening he was covered in a wet eczema. I feel sure that this was caused by the change in the dog's environment. He arrived at the kennels in good condition with no skin problems.

The skin is irritable and the dog scratches and bites at himself continuously. This makes the condition worse so it spreads. The affected area becomes sticky with a discharge and hair must be cut away from this sticky part. We have always found benzyl benzoate a helpful treatment for this condition. The dog may have to wear a hood to stop him getting at the affected parts.

To avoid any of these skin troubles make sure that your dog is given a correct diet, proper exercise, and regular grooming.

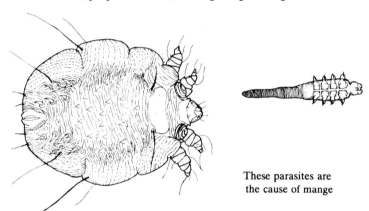

These parasites are the cause of mange

Slavering
A dog that suddenly starts to slobber should be examined to find an explanation. It may be that a small piece of bone has become stuck in his mouth, between his teeth or across his palate. He will probably try to scratch this out with his paw. Usually it is not difficult to remove but your help would no doubt be appreciated.

Snake Bites
Few snake bites in Britain are serious. If your dog is bitten by an Adder, as occasionally happens, take action straight away. A bandage should be applied as tightly as possible above the part bitten and between the bite and the heart. This is done to prevent the poison spreading into the bloodstream. Open up the bite and push into it crystals of permanganate of potash. Then call your veterinary surgeon. Keep your dog as comfortable as possible and stay with him.

Stings

If your dog is stung, try to extract the sting as soon as possible. If it is a bee sting, treat it with T.C.P. or bicarbonate of soda. If it is a wasp sting, treat the spot with vinegar or any mild acid. In both instances it is advisable to have the dog injected with an anti-histamine which will give a quick result and relief.

Sunstroke or Heatstroke

If you intend to leave your dog in his own run outside, you must provide him with adequate shade, otherwise he may in summer suffer from sunstroke. He must always have access to cold fresh water.

The signs of heatstroke are excessive panting with profuse salivation, followed by a general crumbling of his limbs, and then complete collapse. If this occurs, get the dog into a cool place right away and apply ice and cold water to his head, neck and shoulders. (I once saved a well-known champion dog at a dog show by plunging him into a tank of cold water, leaving just his head above the surface.) Keep him in such a position for a few minutes and then remove him to a quiet shady area and persuade him to have a drink. It is quite amazing how quickly the dog will rally if you have caught him in time.

Tails

If your dog lives in a kennel and persistently wags his tail, hitting the kennel wall or door, the tail can soon become raw and start to bleed. In particularly bad cases the top of the tail has to be amputated. (This problem arises mostly with larger breeds such as Great Danes or Irish Wolfhounds.) If your dog has a sore at the end of the tail the best thing to do is to harden the skin at the end with surgical spirit. For bad cases there is a tail guard on the market which is very helpful if the dog will keep it on. Otherwise the tail must be dressed each day, padded with cottonwool, and bandaged. To try to keep this bandage on, adhesive tape and sticky plaster can be used.

Teeth

Dogs should not be troubled with bad teeth if they are given a correct diet. The teeth of dogs may have to be scaled, for which job tooth-scalers are available if you wish to do it yourself. Take the scaler and place the end of the tool at the base of the tooth between the gum and the scale. Draw the tool down the tooth quite firmly and the scale should come away leaving the tooth clean.

Stained teeth caused by distemper or another virus cannot be scaled. They are permanently marked and the stains will not come off.

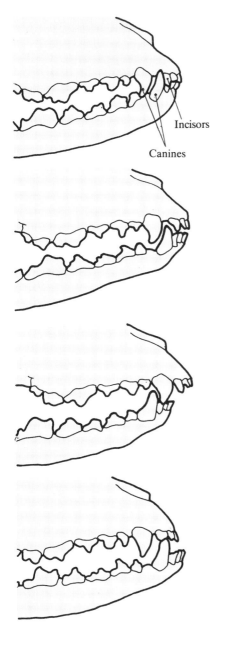

The correct 'scissors bite'. The upper incisors fit closely over the lower incisors and the upper canines fit behind the lower canines.

Incisors

Canines

'Pincer' or 'levelbite'. Teeth of the upper jaw meet the teeth of the lower jaw.

'Overshot'. The top jaw protrudes over the lower, causing a space. The canines are in reverse positions.

'Undershot'. The lower incisors protrude beyond the upper jaw, causing a space between the upper and lower canines.

Travel Sickness
This is quite common in dogs but we have found with show dogs that after a few journeys they settle and get over this problem. So it is best to get puppies used to travelling in the car while they are still young; short trips to begin with, gradually lengthening them until the dog is completely accustomed to travelling with his owner. If the dog persists in being sick there are several good brands of tablets on the market to help him over his trouble.

Tuberculosis
This is not a very common disease in dogs but unfortunately it can occur. The condition is revealed by the dog having a chronic cough. He will also gradually become very thin and have a subnormal temperature. In dogs this is difficult to cure but no doubt your veterinary surgeon will do his best.

Worms
Young puppies usually suffer only from the roundworm. As already stated, these should be eradicated when the puppy is young. Adult dogs suffer more from tapeworm infestation. Whether their presence is suspected or not it is always advisable to treat for them periodically. If no worms exist the medicine will only act as an aperient, providing the correct dosage is administered. The usual symptoms of tapeworm infestation are depleted or increased appetite, loss of condition (particularly in coat), a continual scratching, and a nasty-smelling breath. Treat your dog at once if you see any of the symptoms as nothing pulls a dog down more than the presence of worms. The proprietary brands of worm medicine are effective, but follow the instructions strictly. If you are in doubt at all, seek advice from your veterinary surgeon.

Although roundworms and tapeworms are the most common worms there are others, such as whipworms, hookworms and heartworms that can appear. If you find difficulty in getting rid of these internal parasites and the symptoms linger after treatment, it is probably wise to send a specimen of the faeces to your veterinary surgeon for analysis as the presence of some of the more unusual worms may be the cause. You will need to use a stronger medicine to eradicate them.

Bartholomew Dog-breed Books

The Alaskan Malamute, John Gordon
The Borzoi, John Gordon
The Complete Chihuahua Encyclopedia, Hilary Harmar
The German Shepherd Dog, John Gordon
The Irish Wolfhound, John Gordon
The Pyrenean Mountain Dog, John Gordon
An Illustrated Guide to some Rare and Unusual Dog Breeds, John Gordon

(Uniform with this volume)

The Afghan Hound, Dennis McCarthy
The Alsatian (The German Shepherd), Joyce Ixer
The Beagle, Catherine Sutton
The Boxer, Kay White
The Dachshund, Elizabeth Harrap
The Labrador Retriever, Katya Darlington
The Poodle, Shirley Walne
The Shetland Sheepdog, 'Shiel'
The West-Highland White Terrier, Barbara Hands
The Yorkshire Terrier, Gwen Bulgin

(Uniform with this volume; to be published in 1980)

The Airedale Terrier, Mollie Harmsworth
The Basset Hound, Joan Wells-Meacham
The Bearded Collie, 'Shiel'
The Border Terrier, Frank Jackson
The Cairn Terrier, F. Somerfield
The Cocker Spaniel, Dennis McCarthy
The Dobermann, Margaret Woodward
The Great Dane, E.M. Harrild
The Golden Retriever, Rosemary Wilcock
The Rough Collie, 'Shiel'
The Welsh Corgi, Margaret Cole

Useful Addresses

The Kennel Club, 1 Clarges Street, Piccadilly, London, W1Y 8AB, England.

The American Kennel Club, 51 Madison Avenue, New York, N.Y. 10010, U.S.A.

Dog Magazines

Dog World, 22 New Street, Ashford, Kent. TN24 8UX, England.

Our Dogs, 5 Oxford Road, Station Approach, Manchester, M60 1SX, England.

Pure-Bred Dogs, the American Kennel Gazette, published by the American Kennel Club.

Index